G.G. Smith

The World of Golf

G.G. Smith

The World of Golf

ISBN/EAN: 9783744731782

Printed in Europe, USA, Canada, Australia, Japan

Cover: Foto ©ninafisch / pixelio.de

More available books at **www.hansebooks.com**

THE CLUB-HOUSE, ST. ANDREWS.

The Isthmian Library

Edited by B. Fletcher Robinson

No. 3.

THE
WORLD OF GOLF

BY

GARDEN SMITH

With Chapters contributed by
W. J. MacGeagh, W. G. Van Tassel Sutphen,
and Miss Amy Pascoe

ILLUSTRATED

London
A. D. Innes & Company
Limited
1898

To
ROBERT LEICESTER HARMSWORTH
IN SOUVENIR OF
MANY GOLFING HOLIDAYS,
THESE CHAPTERS ARE AFFECTIONATELY INSCRIBED

PREFACE

THIS book is not a manual of instruction. A man can no more be taught to play golf by a book, than he can be made virtuous by Act of Parliament. But "the world of golf" is wide, and it is hoped that the following chapters may be found to contain some matters of golfing interest not yet dealt with, and to suggest some new points of view.

If, in this way, the book can be regarded as a slight contribution to the cause of golf, the Author, who owes the game much, will be completely satisfied.

TEMPLE CHAMBERS, LONDON, E.C.,
June, 1898.

CONTENTS

CHAP.		PAGE
I.	Golf—Its Origin and Nature	1
II.	St. Andrews	15
III.	Of Clubs and Balls	29
IV.	Prestwick	39
V.	Caddies	54
VI.	The Links of East Lothian	65
VII.	The Making and Keeping of Golf Courses	83
VIII.	Hoylake	103
IX.	The Open Championship, 1897	122
X.	Sandwich	132
XI.	Concerning Style	152
XII.	London Golf	166
XIII.	Golfing Etiquette	181
XIV.	Continental Golf	194
XV.	Twenty Years Since	208
XVI.	Three Famous Irish Links	222
XVII.	Golf in America	254
XVIII.	Ladies' Golf	278
	Appendix	301

LIST OF PLATES.

1.	The Club-house, St. Andrews ...		*Frontispiece*
2.	St. Andrews Links	*To face page*	15
3.	Set of Golf Clubs...	,, ,,	29
4.	"The Cardinal," Prestwick ...	,, ,,	39
5.	North Berwick Links	,, ,,	54
6.	Gullane	,, ,,	65
7.	The Black Shed, Hoylake ...	,, ,,	103
8.	Sandwich	,, ,,	132
9.	A Bit of Old Sandwich	,, ,,	150
10.	Crossing Jordan, Pau	,, ,,	194
11.	Newcastle, Co. Down	,, ,,	224
12.	The Irish Amateur Championship, Portrush, 1896	,, ,,	238
13.	St. Andrews Club-house, Mount Hope, New York	,, ,,	256
14.	Morris County Club-house, New Jersey	,, ,,	262
15.	Miss Amy Pascoe	,, ,,	278
16.	The Ladies' Championship Cup...	,, ,,	294

The illustrations of Newcastle, Co. Down, and the Irish Amateur Championship of 1896 are from photographs kindly lent by Mr. John Woodside.

CHAPTER I.

GOLF—ITS ORIGIN AND NATURE.

THE early history of golf, like that of most other ancient sports, is obscure and fragmentary, while its origin, buried in vague and voiceless prehistoric times, can only be guessed at.

No doubt it all began in a very simple way.

Far back in the dark ages, a warrior was exercising himself with his club one day, in time of peace. Seizing a round stone or block of wood, he hit it so hard and so truly that it flew over the neighbouring trees. After smiling complacently on his club, in pleased astonishment at the result, he hastened round to the other side to search for the missile. Having found it, he repeated the performance, and it is easy to picture him challenging his brother warriors to do the like. Easy also it is to fancy their attempts, the success of some, the failure of others, and the applause or jeers of the onlookers. After the longest hitter had in this manner established his reputation, certain cunning men of the tribe—men who had failed in the far-hitting contests—came to him and said, "Behold! we see that our brother is strong, and that for strength there is none like him. And strength, truly, is a great thing, but so also is judgment, and he that hath strength without judgment is but as the ox that goeth in the furrows. Now, therefore, let our brother hit the stone so that it passes only between these two trees, or that it flies only to a spot which we have marked out behind the trees, and there remains, and lo! we will lay the odds of 6 to 4 against him."

In some such manner, doubtless, was the first game of golf initiated, compact of strength and skill, a relaxation for the warrior's mind, "tired with war's alarms," and a method of keeping his body in condition against its renewal.

Seriously speaking, it is difficult to discover which nation may lay claim to the credit of inventing golf. People have been known to affirm that the game was played by the early

Italians, and there are others who contend that the Dutch are our true golfing parents, sundry works of art being produced in support of both these contentions. The Italian myth has been exploded, as the drawing on which the theory was founded, was discovered, after all, to be a representation of a man slaying an ox, and not, as was at first enthusiastically supposed, the presentment of an early golfer hitting at a ball. The Dutch pictures remain, but it must be confessed that they are more of a testimony to the Dutchman's skill in art than a proof of his knowledge of golf, for the game, as he depicts it, is a very poor affair indeed. In one case it appears to be a sort of hockey, and in another it bears a strong resemblance to croquet, while it was obviously a matter of complete indifference what sort of ground it was played on. In addition, it must be remembered that, as various ancient records and statutes show, golf was played in Scotland at a much earlier date than the first Dutch pictorial representation of the game. Moreover, the Dutch were an artistic people and the Scotch were not, and it is absurd to argue that because the Dutch were artists and made pictures of the game, that therefore they were the first golfers. As well might it be claimed for them that they invented skating, bowls, and many other pastimes, which are represented in scores of Dutch pictures, but which have been common to many European countries for centuries.

It has been said, in referring to this question, that no trace of a hole, the characteristic feature of the Scottish game, is to be found in any Dutch or Flemish picture. This would have been a useful argument with which to support, if not to settle, the case for the Scottish origin of the game, but unfortunately it is no longer available. In a beautifully illuminated Book of Hours, in the British Museum, executed at Bruges about 1510, there is a representation of four golfers, one of whom is putting at an unmistakable hole. Exception may be taken to the player's costume, his manner of kneeling on the ground, and his grip of the club, but there is no doubt about the hole.

I do not think, however, that the presence of the hole in this early Flemish picture weakens, to any great extent, the case for the Scottish origin of the game. It only proves, what is not surprising, that the hole was also known in the Low Countries. But Dutch and Flemish golfers are depicted playing at many other marks, such as pegs, stones, and church and pot-house doors. This shows, at any rate, that in the Low Countries the hole was not *de rigueur*, as it always has been in Scotland, and that the game of the Hollander was a bastard one, without the purity and simplicity which have always characterised its practice in Scotland. There, the mark has always been the hole, the true hole, and nothing but the hole.

Although it may be impossible, from the facts at our disposal, to arrive at any positive finding, I submit that the balance of probability, and even of evidence, is in favour of the Scottish origin of golf. The game has been practised in Scotland, in all its essential particulars, for many centuries, and that with an ardour and persistency unknown elsewhere. If the Dutch or Flemings played any game akin to ours, it seems more reasonable to suppose, in view of their widely different practice and their feebler enthusiasm, that their game was only a clumsy copy of what they saw at Leith and Musselburgh.

Be these things as they may, golf in these islands has certainly come to stay, and the surprising thing is that, with the firm hold it has so long had in Scotland, it should have taken so long to become popular in England, and that its popularity there should have been so sudden and widespread. Fifty years ago there was but one golf club in England; to-day there are nearly 1,000, while everywhere, all over the world, where Scotchmen and Englishmen are to be found, golf clubs are springing up and the game is being enthusiastically prosecuted.

Although everybody must admit the fascination of the thing, it is a somewhat curious matter, when one comes to consider it, this hitting of a ball with a bat or club. So universal and clamorous an instinct must have its base somewhere very far down in human nature, for it has manifested itself in all climes, except, perhaps, in the torrid zone, and in all ages, while advancing civilisation seems only to develop and confirm the more primitive, but still inevitable, tendency. What subtle and potent agency working within us, is it, that hurries us in our thousands to the cricket-ground, regardless of the claims of business and society—not to perform in our own proper persons—but only that we may sit and watch a man hit, with a piece of wood, a round ball hurtled at him by another?

What madness in their blood is it, that causes

obese and elderly gentlemen, who ought to be thinking of their latter end, to array themselves in knickerbockers and gaiters, and to take early suburban trains to inland parks, that they may strike with a club, round trees, and over ditches, a sphere of gutta-percha, and babble of their prowess in the family circle? Surely so strange a manifestation, so overwhelming and imperious in the claims it makes on its victims, must be a recrudescence of some primeval habit of the race, the precise nature and purpose of which it is now impossible to divine.

But apart from this mysterious and metaphysical aspect of the fascination of golf, the reasons for its widespread popularity are not far to seek. With the gradual centralisation of our population, and the ever-increasing strain and struggle of city life, physical recreation, both for its own sake and for the rest and healing it brings to the over-worked mental energies, has become a necessity of existence. Cricket, tennis, football, and cycling, all do their share in meeting this demand, but none of these can compare with golf as a healthful recreation for all ages and conditions of people. For it is not only the overworked city man who has found in golf the health-giving recreation he so much needed. In our country there is a large and increasing leisured class, men who have retired from the active pursuit of their professions, while still in possession of their physical energies. For these men, bilious and bored with the inaction and monotony of town life, broken only by the afternoon rubber at the club, or the yearly shooting or fishing holiday, golf has come as a boon and a blessing indeed.

The healthy surroundings of the game are doubtless another element that go far to make its popularity. Cricket and football are too often played in confined spaces, sometimes in the centre of large towns, surrounded by smoke and bad air. For golf, an open park or common of considerable size is necessary, and of course its original and proper home is the breezy "links" by the sea-shore.

As a physical training, golf is surpassed by no other form of exercise. No other game develops and strengthens, so evenly and roundly, all the muscles of the body. Here there is no dangerous straining of muscle or organ such as occurs in rowing, running, or football. The nature of the exercise is continuous, and calls into active play all the chief muscles of the body, but without violent strain, and, in consequence, the heart is strengthened in a gradual manner, and the circulation improved, to the manifest advantage of all the other organs.

These characteristics which golf possesses make it the game *par excellence* for all men whose physique, whether from constitutional weakness or from the weight of advancing years, has become impaired, and who are consequently debarred from the more violent forms of exercise. Many a cricketer and football player, whose heart or lungs have gone wrong, has found in the pursuit of golf not only improvement and cure for his body, but equal scope for the satisfaction of his sporting instincts. Many a man past fifty, who has imagined that all outdoor games were henceforward beyond his capacity, has in golf renewed his youth, finding himself under the spell of the game, half cheated of his years and his anxieties. It is quite common to hear such a man declare that golf has added ten years to his life.

The presence of elderly men enjoying themselves on the golf links, however, has led to golf being frequently described as "an old man's game"; and this remark is not intended to convey, what indeed would be cheerfully admitted, that it is capable of being played and enjoyed by our uncles and fathers, but the implication is, that it is not a game which any young man should take up, to the neglect of, say, cricket or football, unless he wishes to be set down as a muff. This view of the matter, it need hardly be said, is seldom expressed by those who have ever tried to play the game themselves, and it will probably surprise the irresponsible outsider to learn that no golfer has ever attained first-class form who began golf late in life, or, so far as I am aware, after he was out of the twenties; that, conversely, all the best players who have ever lived or are now alive, have played from their childhood, or at any rate from their teens. As a general rule, experience and history confirm the view that a golfer plays his best game between the ages of twenty and thirty, and usually when he is nearer twenty than thirty. At that age he possesses, in the highest degree, the activity, suppleness, and strength which are essential to a powerful, long game, and a long-sustained call upon his physical energies. At that age, too, he has more confidence in himself, his attitude of mind is simpler, less analytical, than at a later stage, when worldly cares and worries have done their work upon his nervous system.

It is quite true, on the other hand, that, against the decay of his more purely physical forces, the golfer often gains valuable compensation in the judgment and steadiness which come to him from experience and the formation of character. In consequence, many golfers, who have played, and played well, all their lives, only reach their best form comparatively late in life—though this, of course, can only occur before any marked physical deterioration has set in. Mr. Balfour-Melville, who won the Amateur Championship in 1895, is perhaps the most eminent example of this class.

But while golf confers these physical advantages on its votaries, its importance and usefulness as a training for the mind and character cannot be overestimated. In the course of a game of golf, all the strength and weakness of a man's nature come to the surface, and lie bare to the gaze of the most superficial observer. In the ordinary pursuits and intercourse of life, men comport themselves in a more or less conventional manner, so that their strong and weak points are often hidden, even from themselves.

On the golf green, under the storm and stress of a tight match, these masks are flung aside, and we see our own and our neighbours' real natures in all their nakedness. Here, as in the greater issues of life, it is the "still, strong man" that endures. Pluck, steadiness, patience, and self-restraint are the qualities that win the day. The sanguine and excitable temperament, though often found in combination with extreme brilliancy, nearly always cracks under the strain of bad luck, or if the struggle be much prolonged. The game thus provides a bloodless arena, where the highest attributes of human character—the qualities of courage, patience and self-restraint—may be studied and cultivated, and where a man may learn his true relation to his environment, and how to comport himself before his fellows.

But there is yet one more aspect of golf which endears it to its votaries, and that is its social aspect. Like its sister game of curling, it is a great leveller, and, on the golf green, social distinctions are ignored, and all men are equal, or separated only by the breadth of their handicaps. No matter how rich, or influential, or talented a man may be, he is judged on the links by his golfing capacity and his good-fellowship, and by nothing else. Here the simple confound the wise, and out of the mouths of babes and sucklings the great ones of the earth extract golfing wisdom. The game thus performs a great and patriotic service, in bringing all classes of the community together on a common basis, where they learn to know and respect each other, finding out, as they inevitably do on the golf green, what a deal of human nature there is about everybody. The golfing snob we of course encounter, but he is a *rara avis* on the golf links, and, from his position of splendid isolation, is incapable of doing much to disturb the prevailing harmony of the proceedings.

Now that the ladies have taken up the game in real earnest, and are proving themselves such redoubtable performers, there seems nothing to be added to the completeness of the social side of golf.

Talleyrand has said that he who does not learn to play whist lays up for himself a miserable old age. With equal force the remark may be applied to golf. To enjoy golf, a man may begin at any age. It may be that to become a first-class player a golfer must begin early, and have, besides, a natural aptitude for the game; but be the period of his probation long or short, or his ultimate proficiency what it may, he will never regret the happy days he has spent in pleasant places, and he will be thankful that he has embraced a game which, as time goes on, will not cast him off scornfully, unmindful of his youthful devotion, but which will accompany him gladly, making his failing steps easy and pleasant, down the vale of years.

ST. ANDREWS LINKS
(From a sketch by Garden G. Smith.)

CHAPTER II.

ST. ANDREWS.

"SAINT ANDREWS est situé a l'Est de l'Ecosse, dans le voisinage de la puissante cité de Glasgow. C'est un siège de science et d'erudition. La beauté du paysage, la vigueur de l'air y attirent aussi force touristes pendant la belle saison. Et cependant à l'ouïe du plus grand nombre, ce nom de Saint Andrews n'évoque ni une ville, ni une Université, ni un site ravissant couronné par la crête du Lochnagar, mais une étendue idéalement belle de Links verdoyants."

To readers weary of the worn epithets and descriptions of St. Andrews and its links, with which successive golfing authors have loaded their pages, this fresh and imaginative picture from the pen of a French author, will be pleasing indeed. With what wearisome iteration have we not been told that St. Andrews is the Rome of golf, the Mecca of the golfing faithful, whither the golfing pilgrim must go, once at least before he dies; that the Royal and Ancient Club-house is the temple and shrine of golf, the depository of its most sacred mysteries, and that Tom Morris is its High Priest, whose benediction is absolutely necessary for all who would do well in the world of golf, &c., &c.! How refreshing, then, to find an author who, on the wings of imagination, stimulated by a sly peep at "Badminton," can transport us from the region of hackneyed illustration to the domain of pure fantasy. Alas! however, for the poet, as we have often said alas! for the pedant. In his high-souled endeavour to escape the Scylla of effete comparison, he has run over it into the Charybdis (this last is another perfectly unpedantic golfing illustration) of topographical error.

Let us be thankful, however, for the originality of this French view, even if it is not convincing. For to say truth, "ravishing" is hardly the epithet that one can apply to the site of St. Andrews and its links. Historical interest the place has—perhaps too much of it—but it is not a gay place. The spirit of John Knox seems still to brood over the scene, so that on the usual Scotch day it is about as depressing a place as the mind can well conceive, and one shudders to think of what life at St. Andrews would be without golf. One gets a glimpse of it on Sunday, "the times of the sermonses." The decaying aspect of the town, the grey sadness of the sea, and the dreariness of the flat landscape, by themselves are insupportable, and the golfer's heart goes out in sympathy to those early martyrs of the game who suffered for their devotion to Sunday golf. Pat Rogie, John Henrie, and Robert Robertson, across the ages, we shake you by the hand! Not even "the neighbourhood of the powerful city of Glasgow," on the opposite side of the country, can raise the gloom inspired by the ruined towers and ancient buildings, where learning has her musty seat, and not all "the steep, frowning glories of dark Lochnagar," hull down on the horizon, about a hundred miles away, can charm away the air of settled melancholy which the place wears. However, most days there *is* golf, and "golf," as has been well said, is golf, and not scenery—and this is emphatically the case at St. Andrews. There is no danger here,—as there is no temptation, —of the golfer's eye wandering off from the business in hand, to dwell on the beauties of nature. The holes have been so arranged that the very towers and spires of the town, which might otherwise have proved distracting, are utilised as line guides and direction posts, while the hazards, from the sinuous and dirty "Swilcan," all the way round to the "station-master's garden," are horrid and repellant to the eye.

Golf has been played on St. Andrews links from time immemorial, and continuously, as ancient statutes and records establish, since the fifteenth century. The Royal and Ancient Golf Club, or, as its name then was, "The St. Andrews Society of Golfers," at its institution in 1754, fell heir to the great mass of golfing lore and tradition which had been accumulating during all these centuries, and it is to the credit of the club that it focussed and gathered up these traditions and gradually formulated the Rules of Golf. It was the acceptance of those rules by the other golfing societies, some of which were of older foundation than itself, joined to the influential character of the membership of the

Royal and Ancient Club, that gave St. Andrews much of the pre-eminence and authority which she enjoys to-day in the golfing world.

As a school for golfers, the only serious rival of St. Andrews was Musselburgh; but though the latter has produced some champions of renown, like the Dunns, the Parks, and Bob Ferguson; and though that green became the headquarters of four of the oldest golfing societies in the world, its golfing history, from whatever cause, was neither so continuous nor so glorious as that of the Northern city. Which of the two greens supplies the better test of golf is a point that has been hotly contested by the adherents of each school, and there is probably as much to be said in favour of the one as the other, even although Musselburgh has but nine holes. But the fact remains that the latter could not shake the leading position of St. Andrews as the golfing capital, nor has the premiership of the Royal and Ancient Club—during this century at least, —ever seriously been disputed.

No doubt, apart altogether from the question of its merits as a golf links, St. Andrews enjoys, and has enjoyed for long, many advantages as a golfing centre, denied to other places. Though it can hardly be said, in spite of our French friend, to be "in the neighbourhood of Glasgow," or even of Edinburgh, it is still within easy access of both these great centres of population, and Dundee is almost at its doors. While the ranks of St. Andrews golf have thus constantly been recruited from the best players of these cities, the town itself has always had a large residential and more or less leisured population. In addition, the presence of the University, and, what is even of greater importance, the number of boarding schools in the town, ensure a continuous crop of golfing recruits, at precisely the right age to take advantage of the precepts and examples of the crack exponents of the game, who are always to be found on the green.

The continued hold which golf has kept on St. Andrews links is sufficient proof of their lasting excellence, and of the fascination which they exercise on the golfer's mind. A green so old in story, whose every bunker yawns with tradition, whose every hole is replete with memories of "battles long ago," must always appeal to the imagination of the golfer. The constant tread of human feet and the ceaseless thrashing of human niblicks, may have changed the configuration of the ground, as they certainly have caused the disappearance of the whins. But these inevitable results of the march of time, properly regarded, but add to the interest of the place, as do the steps and pavement of an ancient church, worn by the feet of bygone generations. The golf is still as good as ever, and as difficult, though it is somewhat different in character. The passing away of the whins has been counterbalanced by the badness of the lies throughout the green, and if the records have been greatly reduced, it is because the large increase in the number of players, and the great improvement that has taken place in the manufacture of clubs and balls, have resulted, but naturally, in a distinct advance in the quality of the play.

Though the record of St. Andrews links now stands at 71, a reference to the Appendix and the winners of the open championship will show, that since 1873, the average round for the winner on these links is a fraction over 85, while at Prestwick, during the same period, the average winning round was 81½, and at Musselburgh a little over 79. At Sandwich, on the only occasion on which the championship has yet been played there, the winner's average was nearly 81, and at Muirfield and Hoylake on the two last occasions, 79 and 78½ respectively. This would seem to show that St. Andrews is three or four strokes more difficult than any of the other championship courses.

Now, if any verdict at all is to be arrived at, the question of the superiority of any of these five first-class greens over the others must resolve itself into which is the most difficult. Where all are, humanly speaking, in as perfect condition as possible, and where the hazards, putting greens, and tees, have been placed in the best places, as the result of years of knowledge and experience, where there is not 600 yards of difference between the total length of the longest and shortest of them, it can only be a matter of opinion which green supplies the best golf. But if the question be confined as to which green is the more difficult, it may be possible to arrive at a more absolute verdict. Let us see if a further examination of the statistics at our disposal will confirm the apparent greater difficulty of St. Andrews.

In the first place the course is the longest of the five championship courses, and it measures 6,323 yards, or 311 yards more than Sandwich, which is the next longest. Though 311 yards would be a fairish length for a hole of four strokes, it will not be contended that this accounts for the difference between the championship scores. Spread over eighteen holes, 311 yards does not amount to much, and probably one stroke would be ample to allow for the difference in this respect between St. Andrews and Sandwich, and two would certainly cover the difference between it and Prestwick, which is the shortest of the five. How, then, are the missing strokes to be accounted for? The following comparative table may be useful in analysing the matter.

For purposes of comparison all holes from 350 yards downwards are reckoned short holes.

St. Andrews, 6,323 yards.

Long Holes.		Short Holes.	
Over 500 yds.	1	From 350 to 200 yds.	6
,, 400 yds.	3	Under 200 yds.	2
,, 350 and under 400 yds.	6		
	10		8

Prestwick, 5,732 yards.

Long Holes.		Short Holes.	
Over 500 yds.	0	From 350 to 200 yds.	9
,, 400 yds.	5	Under 200 yds.	3
,, 350 and under 400 yds.	1		
	6		12

Sandwich, 6,012 yards.

Long Holes.		Short Holes.	
Over 500 yds.	0	From 350 to 200 yds.	10
,, 400 yds.	5	Under 200 yds.	2
,, 350 and under 400 yds.	1		
	6		12

Muirfield, 5,890 yards.

Long Holes.		Short Holes.	
Over 500 yds.	1	From 350 to 200 yds.	11
,, 400 yds.	2	Under 200 yds.	1
,, 350 and under 400 yds.	3		
	6		12

Hoylake, 5,955 yards.

Long Holes.		Short Holes.	
Over 500 yds.	0	From 350 to 200 yds.	7
,, 400 yds.	5	Under 200 yds.	4
,, 350 and under 400 yds.	2		
	7		11

An examination of the above table and a reference to the Appendix will at once reveal the fact that St. Andrews greatly differs from all the others, both in the number of its long holes and the total of its short holes. It will be seen, in the first place, that on this computation, St. Andrews has 10 holes from 350 yards upwards, while the others have only an average of a little over 6 apiece. Further, while St. Andrews has only 8 holes from 350 yards downwards, the rest have an average of nearly 12 each.

If we add up the total lengths of these long and short holes the difference is even more striking, as the following list will show.

	Holes upwards of 350.	Holes from 350 downwards.
St. Andrews	4,094 yds.	2,229 yds.
Prestwick	2,501 ,,	3,231 ,,
Sandwich	2,568 ,,	3,444 ,,
Muirfield	2,500 ,,	3,390 ,,
Hoylake	2,940 ,,	3,015 ,,

The above figures will clearly demonstrate that the difference between St. Andrews and the other courses is not to be accounted for by the additional actual length which St. Andrews possesses, but is the result *of the proportionate length of the holes themselves.* For in the case of every one of the other greens, the total length of the short holes is in excess of that of the long holes, while the total length of the long holes at St. Andrews is 1,865 yards in excess of that of its short ones.

As the difference between the courses is thus obviously the result, not of actual length but of its distribution, let us look a little more closely at our classification of the various holes.

It will be found, on referring to the table, that St. Andrews has 6 holes over 350 yards and up to 400 yards, while the others have only 7 of this class between them, and of holes from 350 yards to 200 yards, while the other greens have an average of over 9 apiece, St. Andrews has only got 6.

Further, it is in these two classes of holes that the difference exists. In the holes over 400 yards and under 200 yards there is practically no difference between the respective averages of the lengths, and even in numbers they are approximately the same.

Now, of course, it may be said that figures can be made to prove anything, but if it be true, as championship returns seem to show, that St. Andrews is several strokes more difficult than any of the other courses, and if, as some contend, there is a good length and a bad length for a hole, irrespective of its configuration or hazards, it is at least a suggestive fact, that St. Andrews is rich in holes over 350 yards and under 400, where the other courses are poor, and is deficient in the shorter class of holes, from 350 to 200 yards, where the others are strong.

If these figures can be held to prove anything

at all, it would appear that from 350 to 400 yards is a good length for a hole, and that somewhere between 350 and 200 yards is a bad length.

In other words, leaving considerations of hazards out of account, it seems clear, that for first-class players, the most difficult holes are those which present a long approach, assuming that the previous stroke or strokes have been well struck, and I submit, that in holes of this class, St. Andrews has the advantage of the other courses.

Though St. Andrews may thus be held to be the most difficult of the championship courses, it does not follow that it is necessarily the best golf links. The excellence of a golf course consists in the variety of strokes which it demands for its negotiation, and not in the too frequent repetition of one or two strokes, however difficult in themselves. The strength of St. Andrews is thus also a source of weakness, and as all-round tests of golf, some of the other courses, the average holes of which present greater variety in the length of approach shots, will compare not unfavourably with the premier green. The blind character of the going, and its bumpiness, are other weak features in St. Andrews links. It takes a very long acquaintance with the ground to know where good and safe lies are to be found; and this blindness makes play on it somewhat flukey to those unfamiliar with its configuration. The putting greens, however, are excellent and well placed, and the bunkers, though they are of a trappy nature, have not the formidable characteristics of those at Sandwich and Prestwick, and they are not so distributed that long carries are usually necessary for their negotiation.

But St. Andrews is, after all, St. Andrews. Though it has fallen on evil days and is now so crowded up with wandering duffers and schoolboys, that it is sometimes a weary penance to play round it, the old course still has for us an irresistible fascination. It is to be hoped that the new green, which gives promise of being in no way inferior to the old, will in time relieve the present congestion, so that the days of the fine old course may be prolonged, and that St. Andrews, by means of both, may be able to hand down her golfing inheritance, unimpaired, to future generations.

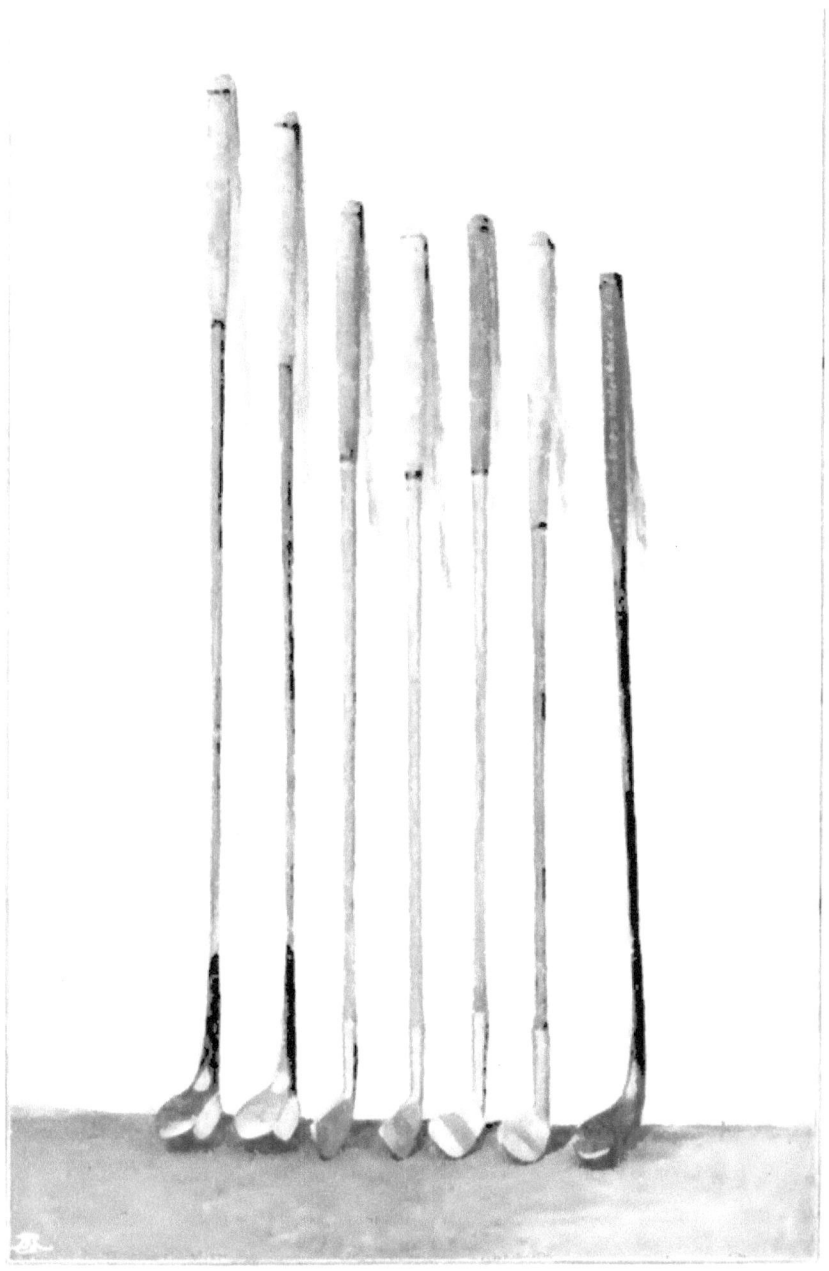

SET OF GOLF CLUBS.

CHAPTER III.

OF CLUBS AND BALLS.

THE golfer is one thing and his set of clubs is another, but it is not too much to say that, in most cases, it is possible to gauge a golfer's capacity by his clubs. There are plenty of clubs about, but good clubs—and by good clubs I mean well-balanced weapons made of good material—are surprisingly rare, and are to be found, for the most part, in the bags of professionals and first-class players. The reasons for this are twofold. Firstly, the good player knows a good club when he sees and handles it, which the bad player does not, and secondly, the bad player, if he does happen to get a good one, soon knocks all the virtue out of it. A golf club is like a fiddle. One may purchase a fiddle that to all outward seeming is perfect, but unless all its parts are made of the proper materials, well seasoned, and harmonising one with the other, Sarasate himself will not be able to make it discourse sweet music. So is it with the golf club. From the end of the shaft to the nose of the head it must be a composite and harmonious entity. The head must not wobble at the end of the shaft, nor must the shaft be so heavy that the head at the end of it fails to make its existence felt. The one should be the complement of the other, the two parts living and working together in power and beauty. Such clubs, as has been said, are rare, even as good violins are rare, and like violins they improve with age and sympathetic use. The late Tom Kidd, the famous St. Andrews professional, and one of the longest drivers of his day, was the happy possessor, during the last years of his career, of an exceptionally fine driver, the maker of which was old Tom Morris. Kidd was a tall man, and the shaft of this club was long, thick at the leather, and finely tapered. The head was long and narrow, as was the fashion in those days, but the face was fairly deep, and there was no lack of wood in its composition. With age, the varnish which had been originally applied on the light beechwood without staining, had attained a beautiful deep amber colour. When Kidd died, the club fell into the possession of an English golfer, who took it to London and kept it in his box without using it for nine years. It was then acquired, in exchange, by a friend of the writer's, and it returned in his possession to St. Andrews. Its new owner was standing on the first tee, with the club in his hand, preparatory to striking off, when old Tom Morris, who was standing by, approached and asked him where he got "that club." The golfer replied that it once belonged to Tom Kidd, to which old Tom replied, "I ken the club fine; whaur did ye get it?"—a remarkable testimony to the individuality of the club and to Tom Morris's powers of memory.

In these latter days, when golf clubs of all conceivable new materials and design have been indefinitely multiplied, and are being daily launched on the golfing world, backed by testimonials from many of our leading players, it is exceedingly difficult for the beginner to know what maker to patronise, and what particular clubs it would be advisable for him to purchase.

The solution of the first difficulty is, so far, comparatively easy. Any good professional who makes clubs, will be able to supply a workmanlike and possible weapon. Let the beginner avoid the shops, unless they be the shops of professional players, for the stock of the ordinary shop is too often composed of the work of ignorant and inexperienced men, and made of wretched material.

In the second place, in choosing a set of clubs, the beginner should eschew all new patents and new-fangled makes. Let him limit his choice to a driver—bulger if he will—a brassy, an iron or mashie, a cleek, a niblick, and an iron or wooden putter. If he cannot play golf with those clubs, it is certain he will never play it with anything else, and he will probably save himself much vexation of spirit.

As above indicated, the first point in a club to be noticed is its "feel." It must be well balanced. When the intending purchaser waggles it, the shaft should not, on the one hand, remain stiff and unresponsive to his call, nor, on the other, should it wobble from the leather downwards like a length of seaweed. The shaft should feel steely and even, through its entire length, and any slight give it may have when the weight of the head bites it, should take place some three or four inches from where it enters the whipping.

The shafts of all iron clubs should be more rigid, but not so inert or heavy that the weight of the head does not make itself felt when the club is handled. The best shafts, both for wooden and iron clubs, are made of hickory, although good shafts are also made of ash, lancewood, greenheart, purple-heart, lemon tree, and a variety of other woods. The very finest, though they are difficult to obtain, are made of split hickory, *i.e.*, hickory which has been split from the wood with the grain, and not sawn off the plank.

The heads of wooden clubs are usually made of well-seasoned beech-wood. Apple-wood is also used, but it is a hard wood, and though more durable, it lacks the spring of beech-wood. In choosing a driver head, choose one that has plenty of wood in it, and one in which the face, or hitting part, is fairly deep. As a general rule it is well to be suspicious of a darkly stained and varnished head. "Good wine needs no bush," and club-makers are but human after all. In a head that has been merely varnished, it is at least easier to see the grain of the wood, and that ascertained, it can easily be stained and varnished to taste. The grain should always run down the neck, and if it thereafter turns inwards to the face, so much the better. You will have a club, if the wood be well seasoned, that will stand plenty of hard hitting. If the grain runs across the neck it is sure to break in course of play. These remarks apply equally to the choosing of a brassy, with the exception that its shaft should be shorter, and perhaps a little stiffer.

Driving cleeks and mashies should have powerful shafts, and there seems no reason, for driving purposes, why they should not more nearly approach the length of the wooden driver than they usually do.

The approaching iron, or mashie, should, above all things, be a handy club. It must be perfectly balanced and not too heavy, and the face, whatever the angle of its loft may be, should be a flat surface from heel to toe, and should not be hollowed out in the middle.

The niblick should be heavy and very thick at the sole. The face is often made too small. Select one with a good large face and well laid back. You will find it of great service in ruts, and when the ball lies merely cupped in a bunker, and when it is possible to hit almost directly at the ball.

Perhaps more variety is to be found in the

make of putters than in any other kind of golf club, and the ingenuity and caprice of golfers have in this matter been fully exercised. After all is said and done, it is difficult to beat the old wooden putter. But the iron putters invented by Willie Park, jun., and J. H. Taylor are serviceable weapons, and an ordinary cleek with the shaft shortened is as good as anything else. The chief points to be looked to in a putter, its appearance and make being secondary considerations, are that it should be well balanced and not too heavy.

The length of club which the beginner should choose, depends upon considerations of his proportions. A man of 5 ft. 10 in. or 6 ft., who has nothing abnormal, either of length or shortness, in his arms or legs, should use a driver whose length, from the top of the shaft to the bottom of the whipping, is 41 or 42 inches. The brassy should be an inch or an inch and a half shorter, and the clubs used for quarter strokes, 5 or 6 inches shorter than the driver. The driving cleeks and irons are usually mid-way in length between the brassy and quarter irons. The iron clubs are made shorter, because being more upright than the wooden clubs, the player stands nearer his ball.

These lengths are given assuming that the clubs are of normal lie. A player who uses a very upright club will, of course, require a shorter shaft than one whose clubs lie flatter.

A set of first-rate clubs, as I have before pointed out, is not easy to come by, and the beginner will fare better in the end if he acquires his clubs gradually, picking them up from time to time from professional players, even if he pays a fancy price for them. He will thus, in most cases, be certain that he has got a good weapon, which is the first step towards becoming a good player.

After exposure to rain or wet, clubs should be carefully dried, and should have some poppy or other thin oil rubbed well into the shafts, and, it need hardly be added, that the heads of iron clubs should always be cleaned after play. A wipe with an oily rag will keep them from rusting.

To preserve the spring of the shafts and prevent them from warping, clubs should either be laid flat or suspended by the neck, by clips similar to those used for billiard cues. They should never be left to rest on their own weight for any length of time.

As a general rule, the fewer clubs a golfer can do with, the better. Very few good players use more than six or eight clubs, and most of their strokes are played with three or four. To become a successful golfer, it is absolutely necessary to acquire confidence in one's clubs, and this confidence can only come of intimate knowledge of them and of their capabilities. The man who fills his bag, as many do, with a multiplicity of clubs, and is constantly trying, now one and then another, for identical shots, will never learn to play the game. Of course it is a good plan to carry a spare driver or brassy, but these should never be used except in the case of a breakage.

The question of what balls to use is not beset with so much difficulty. All the well-known makers supply good material, and it is simply a question of getting balls from them that are of the proper age. It is a great mistake to suppose that the older a ball is, the better, and it is quite common to hear golfers boasting of having so many dozen that they have been maturing for two years. Balls made of fresh gutta-percha are properly seasoned and at their best about six months after being made and painted; but care should be taken that they are kept, during this period, at an even and moderate temperature. If they are kept longer they are apt to become brittle, and when struck the paint will crack off. If balls are known to be a year or more old, they should be immersed in boiling water for two or three seconds before being used. This will do something to soften the paint and prevent it peeling off, but the balls must not be allowed to remain longer in the water, or the gutta-percha will also be softened.

Golf balls are finished with various markings, and at present the "Agrippa" ball, with its bramble-like surface of small and deep markings, seems to be the favourite, though the "Eureka," the "A 1," the "Silvertown," and the "'Varsity" are also popular.

The only sizes of golf balls one sees nowadays are $27\frac{1}{2}$'s and 27's. But ten years ago 28's, $28\frac{1}{2}$'s, and even 29's were quite common, and against a wind or on the putting green, these larger sizes, by their superior weight, were of great use. They had the further advantage of remaking into full-sized $27\frac{1}{2}$'s and 27's, which cannot be done to-day with the smaller-sized balls.

CHAPTER IV.

PRESTWICK.

ON the eastern shore of the Firth of Clyde, a little to the north of Ayr, lie the famous links of Prestwick, famous as the headquarters of golf on the west coast of Scotland and as the scene of many memorable matches. Here, unfortunately, as elsewhere, local records are comparatively bare of references to the game of golf, and it is impossible to say, with any accuracy, at what date the game was first played. The present club was instituted as late as 1851, but the game itself, it is certain, has been played in the neighbourhood for at least a hundred years. A legend exists of a match being played, several centuries ago, on the links at Ayr, "for his nose, between a monk of Crossraguel and a lord of Culzean"; but whether it was the monk's nose or the lord's, that was at stake, or both, and who won, and whether or not the penalty was exacted, are matters that the present writer has not been able to determine.

The chief point is, that Prestwick is an ancient golfing ground, and though the Prestwick Golf Club cannot point, like the Royal and Ancient, or the Honourable Company, to a history extending over many decades, it has, in its comparatively short life, done a great deal to foster and encourage golf in Scotland. Drawing its life-blood from among the active and energetic citizens of Glasgow, and with many enthusiastic sportsmen among the neighbouring landed proprietors, the club soon attracted to its western green all the best golfing talent of the country. The Morrises, Davie Strath, the Dunns, old Willie Park, and many other famous players of that period, in turn visited it and played many important matches over the course. In 1860 the club covered itself with undying glory by originating the Open Golf Championship, when they presented for competition the "Champion Belt," which was won outright by young Tom Morris in 1870, who in that year won it for the third time in succession.

The Prestwick course consisted originally of but twelve holes, and went no further than the wall to the north of the "Cardinal" bunker, but the rising popularity of the club and its rapidly increasing membership soon made a further extension necessary. Eight new holes were made beyond the dyke, and though some of these may be accused of flatness and monotony, they all supply excellent golf, and lend the course, what it previously lacked, the element of variety. The old holes were all of the same character, packed too close together amongst the sand-hills, and too many of them were blind. The course as it now stands, is one of the finest, if not the very finest, in the world of golf. Its total length is 5,732 yards, and its holes of ever-varying length, its formidable hazards of world-wide renown, and its sporting but true putting greens, render Prestwick unsurpassable as an all-round test of golf. For it is not here, as at so many other courses of first-class reputation, that the holes are laid out in one or two stereotyped lengths, with hazards similarly placed for each stroke. Each hole is different, both in its length and in the disposition and nature of its hazards, and he must be a resourceful golfer and have many good strokes in his armoury, who goes round Prestwick without coming to serious grief. Though the roll of famous Prestwick golfers is comparatively small, it must be remembered that the club and course are private, and that, in consequence, comparatively few players have enjoyed the unrivalled opportunities for arriving at excellence which the green affords. A green, however, that was the home of old Tom Morris for fourteen years, and on which, during that period, young Tommy, perhaps the most brilliant player who ever lived, learned to play the game, has no reason to be ashamed of its record. With Prestwick also the name of Fairlie is indelibly associated. Colonel J. O. Fairlie, of Coodham, the father of the present well-known amateurs, was one of the best players of his day. He had the distinction of holding the medals of the Prestwick, Royal and Ancient, and North Berwick Clubs in the same season—a feat for which he was deservedly designated by the Earl of Dalhousie "the Champion Amateur of Scotland." His golfing talent is inherited by his sons, of whom Mr. F. A. Fairlie is in the very first flight of amateur golfers. In Messrs. E. D. Prothero, W. S. Wilson, and A. R. Paterson, the club have three first-class players, who can give a good account of themselves in any company. Since the enlargement of the course, the open championship has been played eight times at Prestwick, and the fact that only on one occasion has the cup been won by a score under an average of 80 for the rounds played, is a striking testimony to the formidable nature of the course. Prestwick has one more claim to distinction, in that it was here, in the open championship competition of 1890, that Mr. John Ball, jun., broke through the long succession of professional victories, and carried off the trophy with the fine score of 164 for the two rounds.

But let us to the course and taste for ourselves its manifold joys and sorrows.

At the very first hole the golfer will find need for the greatest judgment and caution. On the immediate right of the tee, and running all the way to the hole is the railway, over the wall of which is "out of bounds." To the left are whins. A straight first drive is therefore essential, and if it is forthcoming, and of sufficient length, the player will find his ball within an iron shot of the green. To get there, however, unless one has hugged the railway pretty close, when the hole is open, a broken tract of hummocky country, covered with bunkers, bents, and loose sand, has to be crossed; and as the putting green is on a tableland of small extent, with a hollow beyond, the approach must be played with little run on it. Perfect play is necessary to get down in four.

The 2nd hole is a short one, and a well-judged iron or mashie shot, over a small bunker, should result in a three.

The next hole is one of the most famous in golfing geography. It is the "Cardinal," and the huge bunker from which the hole is named, with its wide-spreading sand and high battlements of black wooden sleepers, can be seen stretching right across the course about 200 yards away. Like a black-cowled Inquisitor he sits there, grimly waiting for his victims, and the golfer must have a stout heart who can face without flinching that cruel and merciless presence. Unless there be a strong wind there is but little danger of falling into his Eminence's grip from the tee, and a good straight drive ought to land the player about twenty or thirty yards from the bunker. The "Cardinal" has then to be crossed at an oblique angle if the line to the hole is to be followed. But beware of pressing, or if you have a bad lie, of risking wood. These are two things which the "Cardinal" is always down upon, and if you are guilty of them, it is ten to one that you will descend into his torture chamber, where there is wailing and gnashing of teeth, and whence you will only emerge after being mulcted of many strokes. Unhappy is the lot of he who tops his ball from the tee, and sees the "Cardinal" waiting for him, while he is yet a great way off. Were it not for the cravenness of the thing, I would almost advise him to sneak a bit nearer with the iron, before facing "the presence"; it will certainly save him strokes on a medal day. Close on the right of the second stroke, the Pow Burn waits for heeled balls, but if the second be well struck, an iron approach will be sufficient to reach the green. It must not be played too strongly, however, as there is a stone wall at the back of the putting green. The man whose interview with the "Cardinal" only costs him five strokes, may heartily congratulate himself.

The next hole is guarded from the tee by a stone wall, and on the right, the Burn meanders all the way to the green. To avoid this latter hazard, the tee shot must be played well to the left, when a cleek or iron shot will take the player to the green, if he avoid a bunker placed short to its left. The putting green is a fine one and the hole should be done in four.

The tee for the next hole, the "Himalayas Out," is placed so that the Pow Burn is crossed at right angles. The green is on the far side of the high sandy ridge, from which the hole takes its name. Unless against a strong wind, a well struck cleek shot should carry the ridge and be somewhere in the neighbourhood of the hole. And if we have got well over, there is an element of pleasing excitement in hastily clambering up the sand ridge to see how near the hole the ball is lying. The green is somewhat tricky to approach, and unless the ball actually lies on it, a four must not be grumbled at.

For the 6th hole we now play southwards along the "Elysian Fields." The hole is but a drive and an approach, but the approach is an extremely difficult one. To begin with, unless the tee shot has been a very long one, the approach shot is of a very awkward length, being usually more than a wrist, and not quite far enough for a full iron. The putting green is on a tableland which ends abruptly at its far side and goes down into rough country. Short of the hole, and running close up to the edge of the green, is an impassable country of bent and thick grass. If the ball strike on this, it remains there, and if it light on the green, it is pretty sure to run over the green into the bad ground below it. The hole ought to be a four from its shortness, but it is very hard not to drop a stroke somewhere, and five is good enough.

The "Railway" hole—the 7th—lies at right angles, and with a clean hit straight drive, it is possible to reach the green and score a three, but both to the right and left punishment awaits the crooked.

The 8th is a good four. A long drive, avoiding the railway on the right, and carrying a bunker, followed by a good crack with a cleek over another bunker, ought to land the player on the green, which lies on a slope.

The 9th hole is one of the longest on the course, and the tee shot should be played well to the right, to avoid a trappy little bunker on the left. There are two bunkers guarding the green, but getting short of them with the second stroke, the green should be reached by an iron approach, and the hole done in five.

Turning homewards, we skirt the benty spurs of the "Himalayas" all the way to the 10th hole.

There are bunkers and bad ground to be negotiated, but keeping well to the left, the player should get home with two good swipes, or, at most, with the addition of a little pitch on to the green. Five should be the figure on his card.

The "Himalayas In" is the next hole, and its features resemble strongly those of its brother, the "Himalayas Out." The carry, however, is longer, as the Pow Burn has to be carried beyond the far base of the Himalayas, and a good stout drive is necessary. The water crossed, the green is within reach of an iron, and good putting should result in a four.

Two well-hit shots should take the player to the neighbourhood of the "Dyke" which gives its name to the 12th hole. The putting green, a very fine one, is just over, and, barring accidents, the hole should be done in five. Bad lies, however, abound short of the wall, and its stony face has somehow a magnetic attraction for the ball. In 1893 Mr. Hilton, playing in the open championship, hit it repeatedly, and took ten to the hole!

The 13th is a longish hole over rather bumpy country. But keeping straight, two drives and an iron should enable the player to score another five.

The next hole is by the club-house, and should be done in four, as the putting green is excellent, and can be reached over a bunker by using an iron for the second stroke.

The course here kicks back for the next two holes, both of which are ticklish and require careful play. The 15th is a particularly awkward hole, as it bristles with "blind" hazards of all descriptions, and the green is difficult to get at. There does not seem to be any safe way to approach this hole from the tee or with the second, or at least any one way that is safer than another, and the best thing to do is to strike hard and trust in Providence. The player may thank his stars who gets a four.

The 16th hole is a good one. A long drive well on the left, to avoid the "Cardinal," whose domains are perilously near, will bring the green within reach of an iron, and this, being judiciously played and not too strongly, should enable the player to score another four.

The next hole—the "Alps"—I take to be one of the very best golfing holes in the world. The "Alps" is a high mound guarding the putting ground, but between it and the putting green there is still another hazard, in the shape of a wide and deep bunker. Now it is possible, unless against an adverse wind, to carry the "Alps" and its bunker, and get on the green in two. But the second must be a rasper, and the feat will not be possible unless the tee shot has been also "far and sure." In the amateur championship of 1893 this hole was the scene of Mr. Laidlay's downfall. He was playing in the final with Mr. P. C. Anderson, the game standing all square and two to play. Both had fine drives from the tee and Mr. Anderson, having to play first, elected to play short of the "Alps" with his cleek, in his second stroke. Mr. Laidlay, after consulting Jack White, who was carrying for him, decided to attempt to carry the green with his brassy. His ball, however, was not lying too well, and failing to get a hold of it properly, he slightly pulled it, and lay in very bad ground to the left of the bunker, failing altogether to carry the hazard. Mr. Anderson easily reached the green with his third, which Mr. Laidlay did not, and he lost the hole, and, as it turned out, the championship.

The last hole is uneventful, and unless the tee shot be topped, is usually a four.

Now, played in this faultless manner, our card would read 74 or 75, but, as I stated at the outset, the disposition of the hazards and the ever-varying length of the holes, which necessitate an ever-changing length of iron stroke, make it exceedingly difficult to get round without sundry foozles or mistakes, and we find, accordingly, that the club's estimate of a scratch score is ten strokes higher, or 84! As a matter of fact anything under 85 is very fine play indeed, and the medals are won much oftener by a score above that figure than below it. That brilliant player, Willie Campbell, holds the record for the course, and the figures are worth quoting.

$$\text{Out} \quad \ldots \quad \ldots \quad 4\ 3\ 3\ 4\ 3\ 4\ 2\ 4\ 5 = 32$$
$$\text{In} \quad \ldots \quad 5\ 4\ 4\ 5\ 4\ 5\ 3\ 5\ 4 = 39$$
$$\overline{71}$$

This extraordinary performance has never been approached.

In these "pull devil, pull baker" days of golf, the members of the Prestwick Club are indeed to be envied, in having so magnificent a course as their own private property. A commodious and comfortable club-house, delightful air, and a seascape which embraces Ailsa-Craig, the peaks of Arran, and the noble estuary of the Clyde, make a golfing holiday at Prestwick a delightful experience and an abiding memory. Mr. Harry Hart, who has so long and so ably discharged the duties of club secretary, is all kindness and courtesy to the passing stranger.

There is another golf club at Prestwick, called the St. Nicholas, and the members play on a capital little course of six holes, situated at the south end of the village.

The fine course of the enterprising golf club of Troon, lies about half a mile to the north of Prestwick links. Enjoyable golf is to be had at Troon, and it is the headquarters of that famous and beautiful player, Willie Fernie, who acts as green-keeper and professional. The South Beach Hotel, within three minutes' walk of the links, is well managed, and is a comfortable and convenient residence for golfers.

Comfortable quarters may be had at the inn at Prestwick, but five minutes by rail will land the golfer in more palatial surroundings at the Station Hotel at Ayr. Ayr itself, with its classic river and bridge, and its memories of Burns, is a most interesting old town, and the scenery in the neighbourhood is charming. Though we have no record of the fact, it seems certain that Burns, as a true Scot, must have played the national game. What pity that he did not flash upon it the light of his poetic genius. It would have been a theme worthy of it.

CHAPTER V.

CADDIES.

CADDIES may be divided into three classes. There is the grown up, sometimes elderly, golfing mentor, who is still found at one or two old-established golfing centres in Scotland —the caddie of history and tradition; there is his younger, more modern, and less experienced brother; and there is the common loafer, or the raw and inexperienced youth or urchin who now, owing to the exigencies of modern golf, swell the ranks of the profession.

The old-fashioned Scotch caddie, though he is to-day about as rare as the capercailzie, was a competent and experienced man. Even if he were not a professional player, he could at least play the game tolerably well, and knew all its details to a nicety. He invariably carried for the same players, and the golfing capabilities and

NORTH BERWICK LINKS.

(From a Photograph by Messrs. Hutchinson & Co., Berwick.)

tempers of his clients were well known to him. To many an old-fashioned golfer, the services of his wonted caddie were indispensable for the full development and enjoyment of his game, and the average player would never dream of engaging in an important match without his assistance. The caddie was thus, in addition to his other functions, in some sort the guide, philosopher, and friend, for the time being, of his master, his private secretary, physician, and chaplain rolled into one, his trusted confidant, into whose ears was poured all the golfer's tale of mingled joy and sorrow.

These intimate and confidential relations between master and man were far-reaching in their consequences, for the caddie, feeling his own superiority at the game, and flattered by the august confidences of which he was the constant recipient, ended by concluding that Jack was every whit as good as his master. While this did not prevent him upholding the merits of his own particular masters as against those of his brethren, he came to adopt an authoritative and even disrespectful tone in administering professional counsel or reproof to his employers. He judged his master solely by his golfing capabilities.

"Onybody can teach a wheen loons Latin and Greek, but Gowf, ye see, Gowf requires a heid," as a St. Andrews caddie said to a learned professor at the university, is a remark which well illustrates the caddies' point of view. The fact that they were paid very much according to the wealth or liberality of the players, and that there was no one in direct authority over them, enabled them to develop various idiosyncracies of character, while their unique facilities for acquiring a knowledge of human nature, joined to the native talent for racy and graphic description, made their conversation as entertaining as it was instructive.

On the whole, however, this state of things, though it was productive of much that was interesting and amusing, had a bad effect on the caddies as a class. The constant association with wealthy men on holiday, who, as has been said, rather encouraged than resented their familiarity, had a demoralising effect on their uneducated minds. Though full of humour, they were for the most part improvident and impudent rascals, given to drink, and incapable of turning themselves to any other kind of work. In the winter, or whenever there happened to be a slack golfing time, they were often reduced to the greatest straits, and frequently had to depend for food and clothing upon the charity of their employers.

But the new conditions have changed all that. The spread of education, and the enormous increase in the number of golfers that has taken place in the last few years, have filled the ranks of the profession with a better educated and more self-respecting body of men, though it must be confessed that, as caddies, they are inferior to the older generation. Nearly every caddie nowadays has learned some other trade which he ultimately adopts altogether, or on which he can fall back when no caddying is to be done. Their fixed scale of payment, and their employment subject to the control of a caddie master, has shorn them of much of their independence and changed altogether their habits and character. The surging crowd of caddies, like Italian lazzaroni, that surrounded the golfer all the way to the clubhouse, soliciting employment with shouts of "Cairry for you, sir?" and "Cairried for you afore, sir!" is a thing of the past. At Musselburgh and on the East Lothian coast, the caddies, in making the request, had a curious, monkey-like movement of the right hand, of the nature of a salute. The forefinger was crooked, and the hand was raised up to the left eyebrow, and withdrawn downwards and across the body, with the rapidity of lightning. The nature of the action was not unlike the signing of the cross, and may have had its origin in the superstition of the fisherfolk of the east coast villages, many of which, escaping the wave of the Reformation, are still largely Roman Catholic.

The word "caddie" was originally spelt "cadie" or "cady," and is interesting, being derived from the French "cadet," as one of the many Scotch words in existence which were taken directly from the French, at the time when cordial relations existed between the two countries. It was used in Scotland as a name for a messenger or light porter, long before it came to be associated with golf.

In view of the new conditions, and of the complete transformation that has taken place in the caddie's nature and abilities, it seems time that the existing legislation dealing with their uses was altered.

The Ladies' Golf Union, with commendable enterprise, and backed by the influential opinions of Mr. Horace Hutchinson and Dr. Laidlaw Purves, endeavoured, at the last championship meeting, to do away with the asking or receiving of advice from the caddie in course of play. It is to be regretted that, in quarters that are supposed to be authoritative, this suggestion was received but coldly. The fetish of tradition was again invoked, and it was pointed out that such an innovation would be against the time-honoured practice of the game.

But it should be remembered, that the St. Andrews rules dealing with the uses of caddies, were framed at a time before championships, or competitions with a large field of competitors, were in existence, and were intended for matches, where it might safely be assumed, that the caddies of one side would be in no way inferior to those of the other. These conditions are not present to-day. Caddies on most greens are now divided into first, second, and third classes—a classification which covers all degrees of ability, and all shades of inexperience. It is quite a common practice, moreover, for players to import their own caddies for an important competition, and occasions have been known, even in a championship competition, when competitors who could not afford this luxury, have had to content themselves with the services of boys who had never carried clubs before in their lives.

A player should always play his own game, and most of the best players do. It usually means better play, and certainly shows a more sportsmanlike attitude of mind, but at the same time, all golfers derive the greatest assistance from the services of their regular caddies. A caddie, who knows his master's game and temper, is of invaluable assistance to him in a match. If he knows his business, he will tee his ball exactly in accordance with his liking, be always ready with the right club for each stroke, and have the proper word of encouragement or advice always on the tip of his tongue. In these and in a hundred other ways, in the course of a match, a good caddie relieves his master of a great deal of thought and saves him a large amount of nervous expenditure, to say nothing of the moral support which his presence and sympathy affords.

His opponent, who may only have been able to secure the services of an ignorant and inexperienced novice, is not only deprived of these advantages, but has to submit to the positive annoyance and worry of his caddie's acts of ignorance and stupidity, and how very upsetting these may be, any golfer of experience can well testify.

In private matches, and by mutual consent, there need be no alteration of the existing regulations, but in larger competitions, where the qualities of the caddies must necessarily vary, it seems necessary, in the interests of general fairness to the competitors, that the taking of advice from the caddie should be prohibited.

The difficulty would be largely overcome if it were made the rule, that no caddies were eligible for employment in championship competitions except those of the first class, and if all members of this class had to pass a certain standard of age and knowledge before obtaining their badges. As the rules stand at present, an ignorant caddie may be the means of his master losing the hole or match, or of his being disqualified. The penalties attached to the infringement of certain rules, which apply to caddies, were directed against possible dishonesty and not against obvious ignorance. The awful experience, narrated by Lord Wellwood, of the golfer whose ball lay dead at the last hole, and whose caddie, instead of picking the opponent's ball out of the hole, misunderstood his request and picked up *his master's ball*, to the loss of the hole and the match, is an example of the dangers to which an ignorant caddie may expose his master. A caddie who had passed the proper examination could hardly be guilty of such an error, and it is unfair, in a competition of importance, that one player, through no fault of his own, should have to run the risk of such accidents, which his more fortunate partner or opponent escapes.

The unique facilities for acquiring a knowledge of human nature, before alluded to, which the caddie's profession affords, do not always have the effect of breeding in him an attitude of philosophic calm or cynical indifference, in the presence of a mind unhinged, and beside itself, with the stings and arrows of outrageous golfing fortune. If it be true, that no man is a hero to his valet, much less can the ordinary golfer be a hero to his caddie. The latter, in most cases, sees far too much of the worst side of his master's nature, to have any very exalted idea of his character. All the petulance, impatience, and bad temper of the golfer are displayed, without reserve, before his caddie ; and, indeed, he is commonly made the scapegoat on whom the golfer vents all the vials of his wrath. The caddie has thus need of great patience and self-restraint, and often exhibits these qualities in a marked degree. But the bruised worm will sometimes turn. On a very hot day, a North Berwick player, who had lost his temper badly during the outward half, from cursing his luck, took to cursing his caddie, who, by reason of years and stoutness, was somewhat slow and scant of breath. The caddie stood his master's reproaches and language for some time in silence, but at the far hole, at which he arrived, perspiring and out of breath, some yards behind his master, an additional outbreak proved to be the last straw. Throwing his clubs on the ground, he blurted out, "Ye can cairry yer clubs yersel'!" and marched off homewards, leaving his master to chew the cud of bitter reflection.

Another well-known elderly North Berwick caddie, who usually carries for a certain eminent statesman, of whom he takes entire charge on the golf green, was carrying for him in a foursome. At the last hole, the statesman was addressed to his putt, on which hung the fate of the match, when a man in the crowd behind was seized with a violent fit of coughing. The caddie immediately rushed forward with uplifted hand, calling out to his master, "Dinna putt, sir; dinna putt!" and then, with a glance of withering scorn in the direction of the delinquent, he said, "Can ony o' you folks gie that gintleman a *jubejube!*"

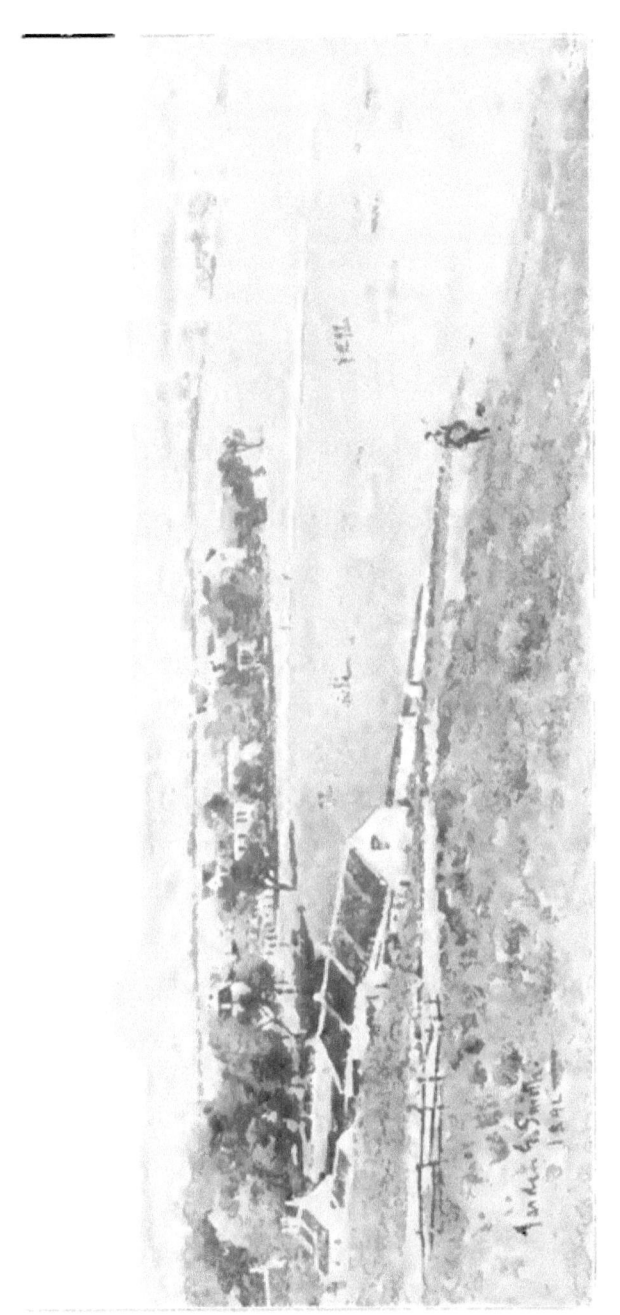

CHAPTER VI.

THE LINKS OF EAST LOTHIAN.

THE country lying east of Edinburgh and Leith, which is bounded on the south by the Pentlands and Lammermoors, and which stretches as far as Dunbar, along the southward shore of what Victor Hugo calls, in a moment of inexplicable aberration, "La cinquième de la quatrième," or Firth of Forth, is one of the most interesting parts of Scotland. From the agricultural point of view it is one of the richest, and the smiling and prosperous aspect of its well-tilled fields, its acres of waving grain or green-shawed turnips, its comfortable farm-houses, red-tiled, and encircled with sheltering trees and well-filled stackyards, amply justify its title to be called the "Garden of Scotland."

In the light of history, no Scottish district is

richer in suggestion, or more stimulating to the imagination, and Scott and Stevenson, who knew and loved it well, have laid in it the scenes of some of their most enthralling romances.

Standing on Gullane hill, under one's eye lies the arena on which many of the most striking events of Scottish history were enacted, and the landscape seems peopled with the great actors who played their parts in it. The rock of Edinburgh, with Arthurseat for foreground, is visible on the western sky-line, and the strath between the Pentlands and the Forth was the channel, up and down which ebbed and flowed for many centuries, the tide of invasion and war. Along here, never to return, passed James the Fourth, with the flower of Scottish chivalry, to fatal Flodden Field. Close by also, in the '45, marched Bonnie Prince Charlie and his Highlanders, flushed with the victory of Prestonpans. From this hill one could have seen the smoke of battle. Tantallon, the stronghold of the Black Douglasses, is but a mile or two away, on the rocks beyond North Berwick, while many a ruined tower and "ancient fortalice," dotted over the plain, speaks eloquently of the stirring times of forays, and harryings, and Border warfare.

Turning seawards the prospect is no less rich in romantic suggestion.

> " The boat rocks at the pier o' Leith,
> Fu' loud the wind blaws frae the Ferry,
> The ship rides by the Berwick Law,
> And I maun leave thee Bonnie Mary."

From Leith to the Berwick Law and the Bass, the waters of the Forth lie spread before the spectator. The Isle of May, Fidra, Craigleith, the Lamb, the Bass Rock, and other islands lie, gem-like, on its bosom, and in the far distance the shores of the kingdom of Fife, studded with villages, can be descried, backed by the Ochils and Lomonds and the Highlands of Perthshire.

Up and down this waterway what strange and ghostly pageants seem to pass! Along here, in the grey dawn of Western civilisation, came the Roman galleys, with their strenuous crews, marvelling greatly at the wildness of the land and the uncouthness of the barbarians who inhabited it. Little recked these bold Romans of a time coming, when those barbarians should bridge this wide water with iron, and when their own degenerate descendants would eke out a precarious livelihood amongst them as itinerant musicians and vendors of ice-cream!

So does the whirligig of time bring about its revenges.

Up here, too, passed Mary Stuart, fresh from the gaiety and light-heartedness of France, to take up, under Knox's stern and ascetic eye, the thread of her passionate and tragic reign. Here, for decades, passed to and fro all the statecraft, the learning and commerce of France and the Low Countries; and "furth of Scotland" from these sandy shores, sailed many a poor exile, either for his own or his country's good.

But the stirring and romantic memories of Scottish history which the scene inspires, though more than sufficient, in themselves, to attract and arrest the interest of the passer-by, are but a small part, after all, of the delights of this countryside. The climate is dry and bracing to a superlative degree. At North Berwick, Dunbar, Gullane, and indeed at almost any point along the coast, excellent sea-bathing is to be had, while the roads, either for walking, bicycling, or driving, are unsurpassed, both in quality and in the beauty of the scenery through which they pass.

The great attraction of the district, however, has yet to be named. It is Golf. All along the coast, untouched by the invading ploughshare, have been left stretches of the most beautiful golfing country in the world. Turf of exceptional closeness and elasticity, natural sand bunkers of endless shape and variety, sierras of benty dunes and saharas of sand, alternating with oases of verdure, make the place a veritable golfer's paradise. Here, surely, if anywhere, must have been the home of our first golfing parents, for nowhere else in the world is the golfing prospect so expansive and enticing, nowhere does the pursuit of the game seem so inevitable.

And yet, strange as it may appear, the historical records of golf are comparatively silent on its practice in this favoured land. Whether the repressive legislation of the Puritans, or the oft-quoted enactment whereby golf was to be "utterly cryit down and nocht usit," in order that the people might no longer neglect the practice and use of arms, had the effect of killing the game for the time, even in its obvious and natural home; or whether it struggled on, like smuggling, in precarious and secret existence through the centuries, there is but scant reference to the game in any records of the district, till about thirty years ago. From sundry antediluvian drivers and prehistoric sand-irons, however, now in the possession of the descendants of the ancient inhabitants, which it has been the writer's privilege to see and handle, it seems probable that the latter represents the true state of the case. A drastic legal measure, the object of which was obviously the stamping out of the game, would be certain to be accompanied by a house-to-house visitation, and by the confiscation and destruction of all golfing implements. What golfer, worthy of the name, to-day, if such a law were to be enforced, would not hide his cherished clubs in bunker or whin bush, and pursue his game when the eye of the law was for the moment directed elsewhere? And this is no doubt what our golfing fathers did in East Lothian. The sudden outbreak of golf that occurred here about thirty years ago was but a Renascence, not a new creation. There, were the ancient weapons to suggest the game, there, was the green; and the people, in whose veins the golfing instinct ran strong, suddenly realised that they might once more play golf, and that no man should make them afraid. And play they did. North Berwick, itself a royal burgh, led the van in this revival of the royal and ancient game, and the farmers of the district reached down and furbished up their ancient sand-irons, and disputed the possession of the links, once more, with the rabbits and "pees-weeps," at Archerfield, Gullane, and Luffness.

There are to-day no fewer than six golf courses, of eighteen holes, in this neighbourhood, all lying so close to each other that a round can be played on each in the course of a summer's day, and in addition, within easy reach, are the greens of Musselburgh, Prestonpans, Haddington, and Dunbar. The six courses first referred to, and naming them as they lie from west to east along the coast, are those of Old Luffness, New Luffness, Gullane, Muirfield, Archerfield, and North Berwick. For a golfing holiday in this neighbourhood, Gullane makes perhaps the best centre. The village lies picturesquely at the foot of Gullane hill, and in addition to its own charming course, is close to the two Luffness courses, and those of Muirfield, and Archerfield. Excellent accommodation is to be had at the hotel, while comfortable rooms can be obtained in the village. The course, though not of the longest description, is unrivalled in the beauty of its scenery, in the quality of its turf, and the sporting character of its holes. Very accurate play from the tee and in approaching is essential, if a good score is to be made, and the putting greens of velvety turf, which the rabbits nibble so close, are the best in the world.

Close by, and occupying the western and south-western slopes of Gullane hill, are the courses of Old and New Luffness. On both these courses, excellent golf of the same character is to be had, though the turf is more unequal, and as they lie at a lower level the views are not so extensive.

Continuing our golfing pilgrimage eastward, the next green is that of Muirfield, which lies about a mile from Gullane village. Though Muirfield is a new creation, it is a green of first-class importance, for, in addition to being the headquarters of the Honourable Company of Edinburgh golfers, one of the most ancient and influential golfing societies in the country, it is now one of the five courses on which the amateur and open championships are played.

The "Honourable Company" came to Muirfield

in 1891, and they must be congratulated on having made so excellent a course in so short a time, out of materials that were not too promising, at any rate in comparison with the surrounding greens. Owing to the rapid increase of play at Musselburgh, which is only a nine-hole course, the members of the club found that it was impossible to play their game there longer, with any comfort, and after much searching up and down the coast, it was decided to lease the present course.

The ground, which is enclosed on all sides by an old stone wall, has long been known as the "Hundred-acre Park," or the "Howes," and formed part of the adjoining farm of Muirfield. Golf has been played on it, in desultory fashion, by the farmers and their sons for years, but no definite course was ever laid out, at any rate within living memory, before the advent of the "Honourable Company."

In the days when East Lothian was a great training centre, the "Howes" was the scene of the annual county race-meeting, and many a famous encounter took place on the course between the crack thoroughbreds of the early part of the century. Old Tom Morris laid out the original golf course at Muirfield in 1891, when there were but sixteen holes. But in view of the open championship, the competition for which is now to be held, with Muirfield as one of the five championship courses instead of Musselburgh, in 1892, the course was extended to eighteen holes. In September of that year the open championship was decided at Muirfield, when Mr. H. H. Hilton won with the fine score of 305 for the four rounds. The general verdict of the competitors, on that occasion, was unfavourable to the course as a fitting arena for championship contests. It was contended that it was too short and easy, and certainly the lowness of the scores returned seemed to bear out the contention. Its inaccessibility from all points was another strong argument against its continuance, while its park-like character, and the ubiquitous boundary stone wall, which waited on the pulled ball at so many of the holes, were generally felt to be against the traditions of a first-class green.

The "Honourable Company," with commendable spirit and enterprise, immediately set about remedying these defects, so far as they could be remedied. By 1896, when the championship again fell to be played at Muirfield, the round had been greatly improved and lengthened. It now measures 3 miles 610 yards, and no complaints are now heard of its shortness or its failure to supply a test of good golf. The new railway, which will have a station close to the club, will remove the objection as to its inaccessibility. The boundary wall remains; but in this respect the course is no worse off than Hoylake, with the exception that, on the latter course, there is cop instead of wall. The putting greens are good and improving, and of large size; but the place is shut in and lies low, and has a depressing effect on the golfer accustomed to the heights of Gullane, or the freer air and prospects of North Berwick. Nevertheless, golf is golf, and not scenery, and the scores made in the 1896 championship are sufficient proof that Muirfield is now a course of the first class, and quite worthy of its place on the list of championship greens.

But a few hundred yards of wood and links separate Muirfield from the links of Archerfield. Archerfield House, one of the residences of the Nisbet Hamiltons, is unique in being the only private residence in the country which has an

18-hole private seaside course attached to it, and indeed, at its very doors. The Archerfield Golf Club, composed chiefly of residents on the estate, has the right to play over the green, and one or two other clubs are also allowed, by the kindness of the proprietor and the lessees, to hold their competitions over it. Mr. John Penn, M.P., as tenant in the autumn and winter, and Mr. James Law, one of the proprietors of the *Scotsman*, in the summer months—both of them keen golfers—have done much for the up-keep and improvement of the green, and are ever kind in granting permission to golfers for a day's play over the course. In these days, when seaside greens are so crowded that it is all but impossible to enjoy the game; when one is jostled on the tee for the right of starting, or places have to be booked the night before; when the green is blocked with duffers, and when golf balls, flying in all directions, put the golfer in terror of his life, a game at a place like Archerfield is a soothing and soul-restoring experience.

From the gate near Archerfield House, which opens on the links, the view is lovely in the extreme. It is "nature unadorned" and full of the simple beauty and pathetic suggestiveness of Scottish landscape. A great moorland-like expanse, covered with whins, heather, and bents, and broken with sandy bunkers and wandering paths, stretches away to the eastward. Acres of greensward lie between, and give ample space for the playing of golf. On the left is the sea, with the rugged Fidra rock and lighthouse, close in. The eastern horizon is fringed with a dark pine wood, and the huge, pointed cone of Berwick Law looks down, over the distant fields, upon the castle and church of Dirleton. The song of the lark and the scream of the plover fill the air, and the extraordinary variety of grasses, moss, heather, whins, and sand, scattered amongst the greensward, make a colour-picture of surpassing beauty. Near the sea, and in a desolate part, is a wooden châlet, used as a teahouse, or for luncheon parties, by the occupants of Archerfield House, and this building and its surroundings suggested to Louis Stevenson his strange story of "The Pavilion on the Links." The golf at Archerfield is excellent. The holes are short but full of incident, and the putting greens are perfect.

Leaving Archerfield, on the way to North Berwick, the last of our string of six greens, the road passes through the village of Dirleton. As one approaches the village from the west, down a steep brae, the cottages on each side, corbie gabled, with "shoppies" giving on the street, and peeps of "kailyards" at the back, have all the characteristics of Scotland. But a little further on, the road opens on a wide and beautiful village green, surrounded by red-tiled cottages with flowers in every window, and as trim gardens as can be found anywhere in England. The huge ruins of Dirleton Castle, full of memories of the warlike Des Vaux and the fighting Bishop of Durham, enclose the village green on the southern side.

A mile or two more, by a straight and somewhat barren road, lands the golfer in North Berwick, under the shadow of the Law.

North Berwick has more than maintained the lead which it gave, in the revival of golf, to the rest of East Lothian about thirty years ago. The royal burgh — an honourable distinction which, as a dependency of the Tantallon Douglasses, it obtained so long ago as 1373—has been fortunate of late years, in having public-spirited and far-seeing men to guide its affairs, and the names of Dall, Brodie, and Whitecross will ever be associated with the rise and prosperity of the ancient burgh.

The place indeed was bound to grow and prosper, although thirty years ago the most sanguine could hardly have dared to predict its present flourishing condition. Its bracing climate, and its situation at the most picturesque point of the shores of Forth, its accessibility to Edinburgh, which the construction of the railway from Drem still further increased, and, above all, its fine golf links, have united in making the town one of the most popular and fashionable seaside places in the kingdom.

There are several golf clubs in North Berwick, but of these only two have a local habitation, namely, the North Berwick New Club, an offshoot of an older institution founded as far back as 1832, and the Tantallon Club, instituted in 1853. There is also a first-rate ladies' golf course, situated near the Marine Hotel, and the greens are open to strangers on payment of a daily or weekly fee. Formerly, there were only nine holes at North Berwick, but in 1877, the course was extended westwards, and the full number of eighteen holes was obtained. These continued in use till 1895, when the ever-increasing stream of golfers, coupled with the shortness and narrowness of the course, rendered a still further extension imperative. Many golfers, who knew and loved the unique and sporting character of this original 18-hole course, were loth to see it interfered with. It has been called flukey and tricky, but there never was a course like it for teaching accuracy, both in approaching, and in driving off the tee. Fortunately many of the old holes have been preserved in their integrity, in the new and extended course, and at many of the new holes, the golfer who remembers things as they were, has at least the satisfaction of playing over the old ground, and with perhaps less danger to life and limb. The wood at the present fourth hole used to stretch some 30 or 40 yards nearer the sea, and this made the course at that point dangerously narrow. Beyond the Eel Burn, which was the turning-point in the old course, new ground for five holes has been obtained, so that now the far hole is almost on the confines of Archerfield. This additional ground has made it possible to lengthen many of the old holes, and the new course, in point of length at any rate, yields to few other courses in the kingdom. Its total length is now 6,095 yards, and whereas, under the old arrangement, at least eight of the holes were within reach of the tee, and many of those but iron or cleek shots, there is now no hole under 200 yards, and the shortest can only be reached by the very longest drivers. The new ground, though it certainly has been the means of greatly relieving the congestion of play on the green, is rather flat, and the holes are somewhat monotonous in character. They are improving daily, however, and the whole course, both as an all-round test of golf and as a charming and healthful resort, is unsurpassed in Scotland.

At Dunbar, still further along the coast, good golf can be had on a shorter but excellent course, and further inland, at Haddington—the birthplace of John Knox, and where golf has been played for centuries—there is also a 9-hole course, about a mile and a half from the town.

The golfer who visits the Lothians must not omit to visit the classic green of Musselburgh. Although the departure of the Honourable Company and the transference of the championship to Muirfield, have diminished its prestige, and though its nine holes are now sadly overcrowded, Musselburgh links remains a grand test of a golfer's capacity. As at St. Andrews, the whins have almost vanished, but the ancient bunkers remain, and, to the golfer's mind, the place is hallowed by association and redolent of historic play and players. If the visitor avoids Saturdays and Thursdays, he will not find much difficulty in getting a comfortable game. Some excellent specimens of the old-fashioned Scottish caddie are still to be found at Musselburgh.

CHAPTER VII.

THE MAKING AND KEEPING OF GOLF COURSES.

GOLF may be played anywhere—that is, anywhere where there is room—but the quality of the golf will depend upon the kind of place it is played on, and the manner in which the ground is laid out and kept. The chosen home of golf, its "most loved abode," is the links, or common land, which is found by the seashore, where the short, close turf, the sandy subsoil, and the many natural obstacles in the shape of bents, whins, sand-holes and banks, supply the conditions which are essential to the proper pursuit of the game. Nowadays Scotland, England, and even Ireland—to name the countries in their golfing precedence—are pretty well begirt with golf links, and there are few suitable spots left on our coast, which the "links" eye of the golfer has not ferreted out, and which have not been turned into golf courses.

The laying out of a golf course on such seaside ground, though it is often sadly bungled, should not be a matter of any difficulty, if a little common sense be exercised, and the first golden rule to be observed is "to cut your coat according to your cloth." If you have about 100 acres of suitable ground available, good and well; you ought to be able to find room for the orthodox number of 18 holes in your round; but if you have a smaller acreage, say 50 to 70 acres, beware of trying to pack 18 holes into it. You will be able to do it, no doubt, for golfing ingenuity and enterprise can do anything, but it can only be done by innumerable crossings, and by using the same ground over and over again in the course of the round. The maps of certain courses look like a tangled skein of thread, and one feels that the word "round" applied to them is a misnomer indeed. Apart from the inconvenience and danger of meeting and crossing which such a system involves, the holes are almost certain to be poor, from a golfing point of view. A hole should always give one the impression that it owes its existence to its own intrinsic merits, to its individuality and character, and not, as too often happens, to the fact that it had to be there, because, forsooth, there was no other place to put it.

If sufficient suitable ground, therefore, is not available to admit of 18 holes being made, without crowding, and in such a way as to use, without abusing, its golfing capabilities, it is better to limit the number of holes to 15, 12, or 9. Better half a loaf than no bread, and 9 good holes are always better than 18 bad ones.

Having determined the number of holes to be made, in this manner, by the extent and nature of the ground available, the same considerations will decide what are to be the distances between the individual holes. As a general rule, a hole should not be much shorter than 100 yards, or longer than 500 yards, while the entire course, if made up of 18 holes, and measured from hole to hole, should be from $2\frac{3}{4}$ to $3\frac{1}{4}$ or 4 miles in length. As I have said, there should be a reason for every hole—a golfing reason—and not a mathematical one. Laying out a golf course is not a mathematical puzzle, and the position of the holes is to be settled by their suitability for the game, and not by the application of the Rule of Three. On a seaside links, there is usually little difficulty in finding suitable places for a succession of good holes. Variety is the great thing to aim at, and here the hollows and hillocks, the plateaus and ravines, the whins and bunkers, and all the other incidents of seaside ground, will be full of suggestions for holes of interesting and sporting character.

To make a beginning, select a point for your club-house—close to which your first tee will inevitably be placed—which is as near as possible, either to the majority of the golfers' residences, or to the station, if the locality be not residential. To have to walk half a mile or more to the club, in addition to having to walk the same distance back, after a hard day's golf, is neither advantageous nor pleasurable, and the cost of driving there and back, adds considerably to the size of the golfer's bill for the day.

Suppose there is a spot 300 yards away from your prospective club-house, either in a hollow or on a plateau, or in some other interesting situation, guarded by a bunker or other hazard, and which would make an excellent putting green, let not your soul be dismayed by the fact that to get there you have to walk through a perfect jungle of gorse. Strong and sturdy as it seems, the whin bush, or forest, if its integrity is once interfered with, soon dies down, and where it flourished beautiful turf can be grown. But before dealing with it, it will be well to consider what hazards are required and what are available for this imaginary first hole.

As a general principle, at every hole, except on the putting green where it brings its own reward, a bad shot should be followed by a bad lie, and a good shot should be correspondingly rewarded by a good one. Now it is impossible, at every hole, to provide a fitting punishment for every kind of bad shot. If this were done the soul of the stoutest-hearted golfer would quail at the number of hazards with which the prospect from the tee would bristle, and all the pleasurable excitement and charm of the game would disappear. But there is one kind of bad stroke which by universal consent must be summarily punished, whenever and wherever it is perpetrated, and that is a "topped shot." The reasons for this are obvious. The shot has been missed and missed badly, but on hard ground or against a wind, a topped ball will sometimes run as far, or even further, than a clean hit one, and the player will suffer no disadvantage from his mistake. Wherefore, in making your first tee, select a spot some sixty yards in front of which, a yawning bunker stretches right across the course, and if it be so narrow, or so shallow, that a topped ball will jump over it or run through it, dig it wider and deeper, so that all balls crossing its jaws will inevitably be swallowed up. If no bunker is to be had, a pond will do equally well, or a railway or a hedge, or a wall—anything, in short, that is impassable.

In the case of our first hole, in burning and hacking a course of 60 or 80 yards through the gorse and grubbing up the roots, all holes will have to be filled up and returfed; but the man who tops his tee shot should be remembered, and for his sake, and for the encouragement and protection of those who do better, you will do well to leave a solid belt of the gorse all across the course, about 60 yards from the tee.

A long driver, when he hits his ball clean, will carry some 150 to 170 yards, and a less powerful player some 130 to 150 yards. From 100 to 130 yards, then, from the tee, there should be another hazard of some sort to catch balls which, though good enough to escape the primal punishment for topped balls, have yet been hit with considerable inaccuracy. Beyond this second hazard the ground should be good for 80 or 100 yards, but guarding the hole again, there should be another hazard which the player will have to loft over before reaching the putting green. In addition, the course may be garnished on either side, according to the taste and fancy of the maker, with other hazards, to catch crooked balls, and also beyond the hole, to punish those that are hit too strongly, but "blind hazards," *i.e.*, hazards which are not visible to the player, such as sunk ditches or holes, should either be rendered visible or filled up.

It is becoming the fashion at Sandwich, and on many other first-class courses, in addition to the penalty for topping, to make the carry for the tee shot so long, that only the longest drivers can accomplish it—that is to say, from 140 to 180 yards. It is questionable, however, if this be advantageous, and whether it does not in many cases defeat the object in view. Against a strong wind, such carries are often impracticable, and they tend to develop a propensity to mere slogging, to the neglect of direction or accuracy, altogether away from the traditions of the game. If two players drive their balls equally truly from the tee, and one, by reason of strength, gets his 30 yards further than the other, the fact that he is 30 yards nearer the hole than his weaker brother, is surely a sufficient reward for his superiority.

I have described this imaginary first hole, not as a model which must be faithfully copied in each succeeding hole. It is to be taken simply as typical of how a hole of that length may be laid out, paying due regard to the reward and punishment of the various strokes required for it.

As has been said, variety is essential in a golf course if the game is to be made interesting, and if it is to afford the highest test of skill. And not only are the putting greens to be of various configurations, but the length of the holes, varying also, will necessitate a different disposition of the hazards. A golf course of 18 holes should contain at least two short holes, *i.e.*, two holes that can be reached from the tee with a driver or even an iron club. A short hole should always be of a sporting character, whether it be surrounded by bunkers, its green but a small oasis in the middle of a Sahara, or if the way to it be so narrow, that only the straightest shot will escape destruction, let it be such, that the skilfully struck tee shot will have its reward, and the miss, of whatever degree, entail the loss of one stroke at least.

It is a mistake to suppose that there are only three good lengths for a hole, namely, those that take a drive, two drives, and three drives to reach the green. These are all doubtless good lengths for a hole, but it is the constant repetition of these distances, and the wearisome recurrence of the same hazards, in the same spot, after each stroke that makes so many golf courses monotonous and uninteresting. The argument for this disposition of lengths, to take the case of the longest hole, is, that the player who hits all his shots clean, is on the green in three, while his opponent, who has partially missed one of his, is not, and has to play a fourth before he is in as good a position. Were the hole 25 or 30 yards shorter, it is pointed out, the man who hits three clean shots, is no better off than he who has failed at one of his strokes, as the latter can still recover his position by playing a longer third. To these Jehus I reply—why not? Is the race, then, always to go to the swift and the battle to the strong? The man may have had a bad lie. Is he not to have a chance of making a recovery? Is the game to be reduced to a dead level of mathematical distances, and the hitting of full shots, one, two, or three, as the case may be, accurately, to be the final test of merit? What about quarter shots? What about all the delicate manipulation of the iron and mashie? According to this theory of laying out golf courses, the good player would never have to play a wrist shot or a quarter stroke, except after he had made a mistake, and the lofter and the mashie are forthwith degraded to the rank of the niblick!

It is no doubt very annoying, after one has played three perfect strokes, and is lying on the green, to find our opponent, after being bunkered, laying his fourth shot, a long cleek or brassie, at the hole-side. Very annoying; but so is a stymie—so are heaps of things. One might as well say that an opponent has no business to hole a long putt for the like, when we are lying dead at the hole! By all means let us have holes of these lengths in our course, for they are good lengths, but let us also have holes of other lengths—holes that will bring out a man's ability to play his iron, at all distances, after as many or as few full strokes as you please, or to judge a running approach, or put cut, or slice, on a high loft, all of which accomplishments are quite as interesting and difficult as thrashing a ball through the green.

The teeing grounds for each hole are important items. Judging from those that are to be found in many places, it seems to be thought that any place will do, provided you stick two white discs in it, to mark it off. This is a grievous error, and the teeing ground should have the care and attention of the green-maker and keeper, as much as the putting greens. The first thing to be looked to in a teeing ground is its situation. It must not be so near the hole, that parties playing from it, will interfere, in the slightest degree, with those playing to the previous hole. Nor should it, on the other hand, be so far away from the hole previously played, that players have to walk a hundred yards or so before reaching it. There is usually some spot, 30 or 40 yards to one side or other of the last green, from which it will be possible to strike tee shots with safety, and if the ground be unsuitable, a proper teeing ground will have to be made. Ground that is on any kind of slope, unless it be slightly sloped upwards, in the direction of the drive, and ground that is hummocky, is unsuitable for a teeing ground. The surface ought to be dead level, and if one has to be made, let it be at least 6 yards wide and as many deep. This will give plenty of room for constant changing of the discs and resting the green. If the teeing ground is too small, and if the tee is not constantly changed, it will soon get knocked to pieces. Two square wooden boxes, painted with the number of the hole about to be played, and filled with moist sand for the making of tees, should be placed outside each disc.

In making teeing grounds, see that they are placed absolutely at right angles to the line for the hole; and that the discs are also always placed at the same angle. Nothing is more disconcerting, or fatal to accuracy, than neglect in this particular.

It is usual to have special medal teeing grounds, in addition to those for ordinary play, and these are generally placed some yards further back.

The extent of ground necessary for a putting green depends on its situation. If it be on a plateau, 30 or 40 yards all round the hole is none too much; if it lie in a hollow or basin, a much smaller superficial area will suffice. In any circumstances, it ought to be of such a size, that a ball played on to it from a distance will have a reasonable chance of stopping on it. The quality of the turf will be a first consideration in choosing a putting green, and spots which are wet, or rank, or weedy, however suitable from the point of view of situation, had better be left alone unless expense is no consideration. It is not desirable, in a putting green, to have the surface flat like a billiard-table, and an undulating surface, provided the turf be equal and true, will make the putting more interesting and difficult. Any abrupt hillocks or ridges which would stop a ball or cause it to jump, should be removed, by cutting and rolling back the turf and removing the soil. If this be done when the ground is moist, and the turf beaten down and rolled immediately, all traces of the operation will soon disappear.

The putting green should be so large that it will be possible to remove the hole to various suitable spots on it, from time to time, so as to rest the green, and if it be too small to admit of this, it will be necessary to have an alternative green somewhere in the vicinity. Many greens are now well supplied with water, which has been done by the sinking of Artesian wells. This is a very costly arrangement, and the results of artificial watering are doubtful. In any case, the ground should never be watered when it is hot with the sun, and any mere sprinkling with a garden hose is useless. Grass will stand a good deal of drought, if it be not walked on overmuch, but if the ground gets very dry, it should be well soaked by allowing the water to flood it for some hours, either very early in the morning, or at night, an hour or so after sundown.

In mowing and rolling a putting green, care should be taken never to mow or roll it repeatedly in the same direction. If this is persisted in, the grass will come to grow all one way, so that in putting with the slope of the grass, the green will be very keen, and against it, it will be very stiff. The holes should be provided with tin or iron linings to preserve their shape, and these should be pressed down into the holes, so as to leave half an inch of turf above the upper rim. If this is not done, and the metal rim is left flush with the surface of the grass, many balls that would otherwise go in, will either run round the rim or jump over the hole.

The greens should be rolled every day, and cut with the lawn-mower as often as there is any grass for the machine to catch. The grass ought never to be allowed to get at all long, and the tips of grass can be advantageously left on the green, where they will assist in manuring the grass and in shading and moistening the roots. Any bare patches or holes on the green should be cut out square, with a spade, and the place filled with clean fresh turf, cut somewhere off the course.

"It is the duty of every golfer to replace turf cut out in the act of playing." This duty, however, is rather to his brother golfer who may come after him, than to the green, for in nine cases out of ten the "skelps" of turf, replaced by hand, and pressed down by foot, do not reunite with the soil. In a day or two they will dry up and wither, and be kicked out by the heel or toe of the first passer-by. In most cases where turf is cut out with the iron, the roots of the grass are left intact, and where this happens, replacing the pad of grown grass on the top, will only stifle and check the growth of fresh shoots. It is much better to instruct the green-keeper to remove all these replaced divots and fill the sore with a spadeful of sand or loose soil, which will be found to encourage the new growth.

For the clearing and making of the fairway of a new course there is nothing so good as playing on it. There will, of course, in the first instance, be plenty of work for the grubber and the spade, and after operations with these implements are completed, and the mangled ground lies before them, the green-makers must be prepared for the reproach which is sure to be hurled at them by outsiders—"Where they have made a desert they call it Golf." Let them take heart of grace. Let but the voice of the golfer be heard in the land for a few months; let his foot, always heedful and tender, be allowed to roam at will over the course. Soon the wounds will unite and heal, fresh grass will begin to grow where formerly there was gorse and bent, and rush and fog, and other unprofitable matter, and the wilderness will rejoice and blossom as the rose.

The foregoing remarks apply primarily to the

making and keeping of seaside courses, and, "except as hereinafter provided," may be taken as equally applicable to inland courses.

It is quite certain that, had the ground on which ordinary inland golf is played to-day been the only available ground for the purpose, the game would never have been invented at all, "and so much labour and much love were lost." Maritime nation as we are, we cannot all live by the seaside, and as we must apparently all play golf, we must take it where and how we can. Roughly speaking, the distinguishing features of inland or park golf, are trees and worms. Now the tree is not, and never has been, in the written history of golf at any rate, a golfing hazard. Bunkers and their like have always been on the ground, and not suspended in mid-air. Therefore, if you have trees on your ground, it will be wise to lay out your course so that they never occur in the straight line of fire. If they do they should be cut down. It may spoil the landscape, but it will improve the golf—and the language. With the worm it is different. He dieth not, and you will have to put up with him, and where you have mud and clay you will have worms and worm casts, and bad putting greens. In the dry weather they will not appear, but whenever it is wet your putting greens will be unplayable. A broad wooden roller, not too heavy, drawn over the greens every morning, will pick up most of the worm casts, but the roller must be constantly scraped, and the scrapings removed from the neighbourhood of the green.

The question of hazards on an inland course, is an extremely difficult one. Sand bunkers of the orthodox kind are necessarily unobtainable, gorse is rare, and hedges and ditches, of more or less unnegotiable character, are their only substitutes. It is usually necessary, therefore, to make artificial hazards, and care must be taken, that these are made and placed with due regard to fairness, interest, and variety. And here let it be said, that whatever the nature of the hazard may be, be it a natural seaside bunker, or an inland hedge or ditch, or a patch of gorse, let there be no doubt as to where the hazard begins, or where it ends. If your bunker tapers off indefinitely into the fair green, cut it square, and to preserve its integrity, build round its face with wood or wattles. If your whins are patchy, and you grudge destroying the stragglers, enclose them all with a white chalk line or a little trench, and let all ground within the mark be "hazard." For an inland course, the only good kind of artificial hazard is made by digging a trench some six feet broad and about a foot deep, at the required place, and at a suitable angle to the line of the hole. The contents of this trench are built up, cop-wise, to the height of about three feet on its far side, and the embankment is turfed over. This opposing face should not be perpendicular, but should slope away at an angle, so as to give a player a chance of playing forward, over it, even if his ball lies close to the face. Wherever it is possible, the trench should be filled with some inches of sea-sand or gravel, and if this cannot be procured, cinders or ashes may be used as a substitute. But whatever the composition of the bottom of the trench may be, it should not be allowed to become hard or caked, and should always be of a soft and yielding nature. But do not be in a hurry to cut and carve the turf of your inland course with bunkers and made tees. Where the ground is park-like, and devoid of natural hazards, it is wiser to experiment with wattles or hurdles, at various distances, until by experience of the course in all states of the wind, you are satisfied of the correct position for your hazards. If this is done, much labour and expense will be avoided.

As a general rule, the proximity of hazards to putting greens should be determined by the length of the approach shot, after good play. A hole that can be reached from a full shot, ought to have plenty of room round its putting green. Where the green can only be reached by an approach after one or two full shots, the hazards may guard the green more closely.

In conclusion, any man who dreams that the golf course which he has laid out will meet with universal approval, is doomed to disappointment. The golfer who plays well on it, will, of course, be sure to commend it; but he who plays ill, will be as certain to say that it is not golf, but skittles. "A prophet is not without honour, save in his own country, and among his own people." There is no green but has its enthusiastic supporters, and none without its equally furious detractors. Let them rave. Look to your putting greens, your tees, and your hazards, and let the golf take care of itself.

THE BLACK SHED, HOYLAKE.
From a drawing by Garden G. Smith.

CHAPTER VIII.

HOYLAKE.

SOMEWHERE in the late "sixties," roughly speaking about thirty years ago, two Scotchmen were spending a few days at Hoylake. One of them was the late Robert Chambers, of the well-known firm of publishers, —a first-class golfer—and the other was his brother-in-law, Mr. J. Muir Dowie.

To these early pioneers the ground known as the "Rabbit Warren," with its closely cropped turf, sandy bunkers, and undulating surface, irresistibly suggested golf, and the possibility of making a golf course, and starting a club, was discussed between them.

They learned that the "warren" was leased, along with the neighbouring farm, to one, John Ball, the landlord of the local hotel, and our two Scotchmen accordingly approached him and laid their views before him. Mr. Ball was then a stalwart yeoman of thirty-six years, and being a keen sportsman, though he knew nothing of the Scottish game, he was good enough to fall in with the views of the strangers, and to grant them permission to cut nine little round holes, and stick nine little red flags in them.

This was the beginning of things at Hoylake.

A room in the hotel was obtained as a club-room, and the club was started with about a dozen members, and jogged along comfortably for many years, in great contentment and with much good-fellowship. In the meantime, honest John himself had taken to the game, and exhibited such aptitude for it, in spite of a style that was somewhat unorthodox, as to suggest that his name must have come to him from some remote ancestor of ball-hitting propensities. Few could beat him in these years. He played against his master and first instructor, Mr. Chambers, in a match against the Tantallon Golf Club, and beat him by four holes; and in the amateur championship of 1887, at Hoylake, he only succumbed at the last hole, in the semi-final round, to Mr. H. G. Hutchinson. But whether Mr. Ball derived his aptitude for hitting a golf ball from his forefathers or not, there can be no doubt that he transmitted his own skill to his son, whose name is also John, and who began to play at Hoylake, in emulation of his elders, when he was about six years old. John Ball, "tertius," as he was then styled, and now "junior," or more shortly "Johnnie," had many opportunities as a child, and as he grew up, of seeing golf "as she should be played." Young Tom Morris, Davie Strath, and Jamie Allan, played many matches over the links, and no future champion could have wished for finer golfers to fire his youthful ardour, or better models on which to form his style. Everybody knows what use he made of his opportunities, and how, after being four times amateur champion, and once open champion, he is to-day one of the prettiest, as he is certainly one of the very best golfers in the world.

With the rise and supremacy of Johnnie Ball, the Hoylake Club and links gained ever-increasing renown and popularity. Members joined in large numbers from all parts of the country. The course was enlarged and improved, the club had new premises built on to the hotel, and Hoylake became the flourishing centre of English golf. In 1882, the club had the good fortune to secure the services of Mr. Thomas Owen Potter as honorary secretary, and to his able management, a great deal of the success of the Royal Liverpool Golf Club, and of the popularity which golf now enjoys in England, must be attributed. As a cricketer, Mr. Potter was well known, having played for Lancashire, and on taking up golf, he brought to the discharge of his duties as honorary secretary, all the enthusiasm and geniality of a genuine English sportsman. Every passing golfer who visited Hoylake, during the thirteen years of his tenure of office, took away with him something of his enthusiasm for the game, of his kindliness and good-fellowship; and to the seeds so spread, to his advice and help, always ungrudgingly given, many golf clubs owe their present existence and prosperity. May he long live to view, in his retirement, the fruits of his labours.

When Johnnie Ball was in his teens, a small, fair-haired child called Hilton, used to watch him playing on the green. As he grew up, this child exhibited astonishing proficiency at the game. He won the boys' medal at Hoylake four times; the first time when he was only ten years of age. So rapidly did he progress, that at last "Johnnie" himself, could not give him anything, and a beating; and though he has not yet won the amateur championship, he has been the "runner-up" on three occasions. But in 1892, at Muirfield, he attained the distinguished honour of winning the open championship, with the marvellous score of 305 for 72 holes; and this year he has again secured the coveted distinction, on his own green, with the grand score of 314.

Mr. J. Graham, jun., is another young Hoylake player of first-class ability, of whom more will be heard; and there are others coming on who bid fair to maintain the reputation of Hoylake golf. The local professional, also a native of the place, George Pulford, tied in this year's (1897) championship with Mr. Tait for the third place, and he has shown, on many occasions, that he is quite able to hold his own with the best of them.

Altogether it is a remarkable phenomenon, this school of Hoylake golf. With the exception of Mr. Horace Hutchinson, no English amateur has, so far, attained first-class honours outside the charmed circle of Hoylake, and Mr. Hutchinson is a cosmopolitan golfer, and has played as much at Hoylake as anywhere else. Were one to pick a team of amateurs to represent England, it would be almost entirely composed of Hoylake players. To have taken up the game so lately, and to maintain as they do, more than successfully, their equality with the pick of Scottish players at their own national game, is an achievement of which the golfers of Hoylake may well be proud.

Doubtless, at Hoylake, many circumstances unite to favour and foster the successful pursuit of the game. Its situation, close to Liverpool, and midway between Scotland and the Metropolis, makes it a convenient centre for golfers from all parts, and renders it by far the most suitable green, from the point of view of locality, for championship competitions. The course itself is superb, and the wealth and virility of the club are testified by the excellent condition in which the green is maintained, and by the number of club competitions and the keenness with which they are contested. The course is surrounded by the houses of Hoylake and West Kirby, inhabited by well-to-do people, most of whom play the game from their earliest years, and who have only to step out of their front doors to be on the green.

In these respects, in addition to its excellent

climate, Hoylake enjoys advantages which are denied to many other first-class greens. Neither Prestwick, nor Sandwich, nor Westward Ho! are residential in the same sense, and their distance from any great centre of population, precludes the possibility of their ever producing any great golfing hierarchy. The only green where the necessary conditions are present, to anything like the same extent, is St. Andrews, and it is to St. Andrews, which has produced so many grand golfers in the past, that Scotchmen look to reassert the ancient supremacy of Scottish golf.

A golfing holiday at Hoylake, if the weather be normal, is sure to be one of unalloyed pleasure. At the Royal Hotel, the golfer will be most comfortably housed and fed, and he will be sure to find congenial golfing society. There also he will find Mr. T. Owen Potter, the late honorary secretary of the club, who has his quarters in the hotel, and in the bar parlour, after dinner, with Mr. Ball, sen., and Mr. Potter in the chair, many pleasant half-hours are to be spent, over the pipes and "'baccy," with tales and reminiscences of golf and golfers.

The 17th hole is at the door, and right opposite is the palatial new club-house. Mr. Ryder Richardson, the secretary, Mr. Potter's courteous and efficient successor, will smooth the path of the visitor, and he will find amongst the members, a cordiality, and a north-country sincerity and hospitality, which are equalled nowhere.

The caddies of Hoylake, fishermen for the most part, or sons of fishermen, under the eye of Jack Morris, and the able management of Hughes, have developed into a very satisfactory body. Though a good many of them are undersized, they all take a keen interest in the game, and many of them are very good players.

The course at Hoylake has undergone several changes in recent years, the most important alteration being the addition of two new holes after the "Cop," called respectively the "Telegraph" and the "Briars," which addition was rendered necessary by the absorption of the old third hole, by the extension of building west of the new club-house. Though somewhat rough at present, these new holes give promise, by their sporting character, of being a great acquisition to the course.

The present first hole, was the old second, before the new club-house was built, and the path to it, to those who are unfamiliar with the course, is perplexing in the extreme. From the medal or championship tee—and it will be understood that in dealing with the rest of the course these tees are implied—it takes a full drive, even on a quiet day, to get round the corner of the field, and the drive must be absolutely straight. The field on the right, if one reaches so far, is out of bounds, and entails a distance penalty for all balls getting into it; and on the left are gardens, cops, sand, and other hazards to catch the "pulled." Between the Scylla of the field and the Charybdis of garden, cop, and bunker, there is but a narrow way, and the ground, though flat to outward seeming, has a most treacherous fall to either side, so that a running shot, unless after a long carry, never goes straight on, but inevitably rolls off, either to the ditch round the field, on the right, or to the hazards on the left. But assuming that the tee shot lies, where it ought to be, on the fair course, some yards past the corner of the field, a shot no less difficult remains to be played. The flag appears to be still a long way off, on the flat, with no bunker intervening, and nothing to guide the eye but the narrowing perspective of the ditch on the right and the rabbity country on the left. Absolute straightness is again essential. Experience alone will teach the strength, but everybody goes too far in the first instance. The putting green is a fine one, but he who holes in four, has done well.

The 2nd hole—the "Road"—lies at right angles, to the left. A good drive, slightly to the right, will give the best approach to the hole. The green lies in a corner, backed by the turnpike road and a field, both of which are "out of bounds." A bunker guards the green on the left, and the player, by playing his tee shot to the right, avoids the necessity of carrying this, and gives himself a longer run for his approach shot. This hole should be done in four.

Teeing alongside the cop, over which is out of bounds, and which, with its inevitable ditch, accompanies us all the way on the immediate left, we face the "Long" hole. On the right, with about 60 yards between, another ditch runs parallel with the cop, all the way to the green. About 200 yards from the tee, a wide bunker stretches right across the course, and fully 200 yards further on, a similar hazard guards the putting green. If the wind be behind the player, he will be wise, who plays his cleek or driving mashie from the tee, for even a moderate shot from a wooden club will here run a very long way, and most likely finish up in the first bunker. A well-hit cleek shot will take the player very near it, and then he can take his driver, and hit his second, for all he is worth, towards the second bunker. There is not much danger of his reaching that. An iron pitch across, steady putting, and the hole is done, simply, in five, and occasionally in four, if the wind be favourable. All that is wanted is straight hitting.

The next hole is the "Cop." This is a short hole of 140 yards or thereabouts, but a very accurate tee shot is required if a three is to be recorded. About six yards in front of the tee runs the cop, to catch a topped or insufficiently lofted ball; on the left runs another cop, and immediately in front of the green, and right across it, a bunker waits for short balls.

In all states of the wind, a high shot is essential at this hole. It is true there is a telegraph wire overhead, but the cop below is worse.

We now play the first of the new holes, and here we encounter, amongst other things, not only the wire, but a very substantial telegraph post as well. A good tee shot, slightly on the

I

right, will carry the ball to a good lie, over some very nasty country, bristling with gorse, ditches, and bunkers, and will leave the player a long carry to the green, over a sandy ridge, on which runs the telegraph. The green is as yet coarse and rough, and the hole is a good five.

The next is another new hole, called the "Briars," and is one of the most sporting holes to be found anywhere. To top the tee shot, is to land in unnegotiable gorse. To heel, is good-bye to a four; and to pull, is to land out of bounds amongst trees and shrubbery. The tee shot must be high, and played well over the left of the trees, if the green is to be reached in two, for that is the straight line to the hole. If the corner of the trees only is carried, there is every chance of the ball lying badly amongst the hillocks and bunkers which nature and man have scattered, in rich profusion, about 50 yards beyond, and, in any case, to take this line entails a very long and difficult second. By playing his first stroke well on the left, the player should have no difficulty in carrying the bunker guarding the green, when he has a good chance of a four.

The 7th, or "Dowie" hole—named after one of the founders of the course—brings us back to the old course. This is another shortish hole of 190 yards, and the hole is cut on a green close to the "out-of-bounds" field, which runs almost parallel to the line of fire, and which is bounded by a cop and ditch. A pulled ball is therefore fatal, unless it has been played well to the right, in which case it is perhaps the best stroke possible, as it will enable the player to avoid the patches of rushes which guard the immediate approach to the hole. The putting green is small and very keen, and though the hole should be done in three, four is quite good enough.

Continuing, with the cop and "out of bounds" still threatening us on our left, and eschewing a "pull," we hit off for the "Far" hole. Here again one must be absolutely straight, for on the right are innumerable small hollows and hillocks, which will prevent the possibility of getting away a long second. The second stroke must be played to the right, to avoid a vast hidden bunker which gapes on the left for the unwary. The approach is difficult, and wants knowing, and the putting green is on a slope. This hole is a very good five.

We now turn homewards, and climbing to the tee for the "Punchbowl," we get our first and only glimpse of the sea—that is, if the tide be in. If it is low water, nothing but a barren waste of sand stretches to the horizon, but the golfer can rest and refresh his eye with the magnificent panorama of the Welsh hills, rising beyond the waters of the Dee. The tee shot for the "Punchbowl" must be a long one, and, moreover, unless it carry the half-way ridge, it must be on the left, for on the face of the ridge are two nasty pocket-like bunkers, one behind the other, and to the right of them again is the abomination of desolation. Giving the pocket-bunkers a wide berth on the left, a fairish lie is probable, and the green can be reached with the second stroke. Should the ball pitch short, however, there is little likelihood of its getting over the second ridge, and it will most probably be found either in another bunker at its base, or in one of the small hard holes with which the ground is here honeycombed. If the player holes out here in five and is out—for this is the 9th hole—in forty, he has played very sound golf.

Another long tee shot is required at the 10th hole, for unless the player carry well over the ridge, he will not be able to get home in two, and will most likely have a hanging lie in sandy ground. With a tee shot of sufficient length the hole presents no other difficulty, and it should be done in four.

The 11th, or "Alps" hole, formerly made, with the present 10th, one of the longest holes on the course. It is now only a full drive, but it must be a good and straight one, and sufficiently high to carry the hill in front of the green. This is one of the prettiest holes to be found anywhere, and the putting green is beautiful and very true. A three is very useful at this hole.

The 12th hole—the "Hilbre"—is almost a repetition of the 10th. A straight drive and a long run up the flat to the green, will result in a four, but care must be taken not to overrun the hole, beyond which are rushes and a pool of water.

Only 80 or 90 yards lie between the tee and the next hole—the "Rushes"—but the intervening ground is rushes all the way, and terminates in a bunker, surmounted by a cop, directly behind which the hole is cut. A high shot with a pitching iron, played to fall as dead as possible, is required here, and if it comes off, a refreshing two may possibly be obtained.

If a player's score is going to be a good one, it ought at this point to be looking fairly healthy, for there is not much chance of his improving it in the remaining five holes. If he gets home in twenty-five he will have done very well, for he will have his work cut out to avoid an occasional six, or even worse. They are all long holes, averaging 400 yards, and make a very punishing finish to the round.

Two long drives played right up the course, and without attempting to cross with the second shot, either the ditch on the right or the bunker in front, will take the player within a cleek or iron shot of the 14th, or "Field" hole. The approach should be played to the left of the hole, and the player ought to be content with a five. If he plays straight on the hole his ball will most likely be caught in the rushes in front of the green, or roll beyond into the ditch.

With a following wind it is possible to reach the green of the 15th, or "Lake" hole, in two strokes, but they must be rakers, and a five will not be amiss at this hole. There are some nasty lies to be had on the way, especially on the right, where the rabbits have a large settlement, and in the neighbourhood of the green. A tee shot played straight on the hole will have the best chance of good treatment, and will, besides, open the hole better than any other line.

The next hole—the "Dun"—is one of the most difficult holes on the course. It is now about 100 yards longer than it used to be, and whether they play their second strokes past the corner of the field, or more greatly daring, carry over it, straight for the green, players cannot reach the green in less than three strokes. The approach is very difficult, over a most deceptive bunker, with the hole so near it that it is almost impossible to avoid running past. This hole is an excellent five.

The 17th hole—the "Royal"—although a fair length, presents no special difficulties, and should be reached in two strokes, and holed in four.

The last hole is another long hole, and only with the wind behind is it at all easy to carry the bunker in front of the hole, with the second stroke. Here, however, there is plenty of room between the bunker and the hole, and with steady play the hole should be done in five strokes.

There can be no question that the course of the Royal Liverpool Club affords a magnificent test of golf. Here, as at all other championship courses, the long driver will gain many strokes in the round over his less powerful opponent, while at the same time there are plenty of opportunities for the display of dexterity with the use of the iron or mashie, at all distances, and for every variety of quarter stroke. Of course Hoylake has its weak points, like every other first-class green. It is the opinion of J. H. Taylor, twice open champion, that the soil is too hard, and it was at all events pretty generally agreed amongst the professionals at the open championship, that the course takes a deal of knowing. A great many of the holes are so placed, at the end of long, flat stretches, without any guide, half or three-quarter way, in the shape of a bunker or other hazard, to assist the eye, that the judging of distance accurately, is only possible after long experience, in all states of the weather.

Other weak points in the course are, the almost invariable punishment that overtakes a pulled ball and the almost complete immunity enjoyed by the heeled. At nearly every hole a ball, if only slightly pulled, will land either out of bounds or in a very bad country, while the heeled, and the badly heeled at that, will go skipping merrily along, over grassy slopes, to rest on good lies, and will never be out of bounds, except at the 1st and 16th holes. These things, of course, are unavoidable, owing to the surroundings and configuration of the ground, though they remain exasperating characteristics of Hoylake.

In spite of its length, which is practically equal to that of the other championship courses, Hoylake would appear, judging from the winning scores at the open championship competitions, to be a few strokes easier than either Prestwick, Sandwich, or St. Andrews, and from the point of view of difficulty, is apparently about the same as Muirfield. This is no doubt to be accounted for, by the fact that the carries from the tee, and throughout the green, have not the daunting aspect of those at Sandwich or the northern courses, and the consequences of mistakes are not here so appalling and irreparable. Yet, taking one thing with another, and in spite of all that may be said against it, the golfer will go far, before he finds a better green, or better fellows, than Hoylake and its players.

CHAPTER IX.

THE OPEN CHAMPIONSHIP, 1897.

LOVELY summer-like weather prevailed at Hoylake, in the month of May, for the week in which, for the first time on this course, the open championship was played. Cloudless skies overhead, and the hot sun tempered by a gentle easterly breeze, that eased the outward journey and did not seriously impede the homeward, made the weather conditions perfect, for players and spectators alike. The course was in first-rate order, if a trifle on the hard side, and the putting greens, especially, would have been much improved by a day's rain.

For a few days previous to the event, the combatants had been gathering from near and from far. Professional competitions, organised during the previous week by the neighbouring clubs at

Wallasey and Southport, helped to relieve the monotony of practice at Hoylake, and the results of these were eagerly scanned, as affording some index of the prevalent form of the players.

The championship fell to be played on the Wednesday and Thursday, but by the Sunday previous, almost all the competitors, of whom there were 88, were at Hoylake, and all day long—there being no Sunday play at Hoylake—the links were dotted over with little groups of golfers, inspecting the course, and discussing the probabilities of the coming event. At the "Old Alps," quite early, was a group comprised of Mr. J. E. Laidlay, Mr. C. Hutchings, Mr. H. H. Hilton, Andrew Kirkaldy, J. H. Taylor, W. Auchterlonie, J. Kay, the two Simpsons, and Willie Park—a pretty strong galaxy of golfers. Andrew Kirkaldy, though he had not yet played over the course, expressed the opinion that the putting greens "were jist the kin' that he liked"; and how accurately he had diagnosed their suitability for himself, he proved, next morning, by going round in 76. Taylor had done a 73 the previous week, but he now seemed a bit off colour, and ascribed that marvellous performance to luck on the greens. He and the other professionals seemed to fancy most the chances of Harry Vardon, last year's champion, who had been first at Southport, the previous day, and who was in magnificent form. Mr. Hilton, who knows Hoylake and its possibilities better perhaps than any other player, gave it as his opinion, that two 79's and two 80's, would win, and that while an individual score of 76 might be returned, two rounds of 75 would not be done throughout the competition. Little he recked, as he stood there, that he was to prove, in his own proper person, the falsity of his predictions in each particular. But we must not anticipate. Willie Park and Mr. Laidlay were engaged in an animated discussion on putting, in which department of the game they both found themselves, for the moment, out of form, and were administering to each other, sundry hints and prescriptions, for their respective varieties of this distressing malady. Elsewhere, were to be seen the two Vardons, with their finely cut features and fists like legs of mutton, and the stalwart form of Braid, towering above a group in which were cheery Ben Sayers from North Berwick, and Davie Brown and Willie Fernie, two former champions. With the exception of Mr.

H. Hutchinson and Douglas Rolland no golfing figure of note was absent. In the club-house, the chances of the amateurs were favourably entertained. With Mr. Ball and Mr. Hilton playing on their own green, with Mr. Tait, Mr. Laidlay, and Mr. Mure Fergusson all to the fore, it was felt that the professionals would not have things all their own way, as had so often previously been the case.

Monday and Tuesday were again glorious days, though Jack Morris's prayers for rain remained unanswered, and the putting greens became more and more fiery. From morning till night the air was alive with the crack of clean-hit balls, and some excellent scores were made in practice, though Andrew Kirkaldy's score of 76 on Monday morning, was not beaten before Wednesday, when the competition opened.

The first round produced nothing sensational in the way of scores. Mr. John Ball and A. Herd returned cards of 78 each; Mr. Tait and Davie Brown 79 each; and Mr. Hilton, J. Braid, and G. Pulford took 80. Mr. Laidlay and J. H. Taylor were 82 each, Harry Vardon 84, while Willie Park put himself completely out of the running with a 91.

The afternoon saw the best all-round play of the competition. Mr. Hilton returned a magnificent card of 75, which was immediately surpassed by a 74—an absolutely perfect score—by J. Braid. Ben Sayers greatly improved his position with a 78. Mr. Tait again did 79, a score which was equalled by G. Pulford, Peter McEwan, and T. Renouf.

The results of the first day's play left the competition a very open one, and was remarkable in that three amateurs were to be found in the first six. The following list shows the respective scores of the first six :—

J. Braid	80	74 = 154
Mr. H. H. Hilton	80	75 = 155
Mr. F. G. Tait	79	79 = 158
G. Pulford	80	79 = 159
Mr. John Ball	78	81 = 159
A. Herd	78	81 = 159

The first round on Thursday—another perfect day—seemed to be, on the face of it, a disastrous one for the two leaders, for Mr. Hilton took 84, and J. Braid 82. Mr. Ball spoiled his chance with an 88. Pulford, Herd, and Mr. Tait improved their positions with two 79's and an 80, respectively, so that, at the completion of the third round, the position of the leaders was as follows :—

	1st Day's Score.	
J. Braid	154 ...	82 = 236
Mr. F. G. Tait	158 ...	80 = 238
G. Pulford	159 ...	79 = 238
A. Herd	159 ...	79 = 238
Mr. H. H. Hilton	155 ...	84 = 239

All this promised a close and exciting finish, and the onlookers were not disappointed in this respect. Mr. Tait was the first of the likely ones to finish his fourth round. By steady and beautiful golf, he handed in another score of 79, bringing his grand aggregate to 317; and this score, in the opinion of many, gave him a very strong position. This fine score, however, was not long allowed to go unchallenged. It was soon reported that Mr. Hilton was playing in surprising form. Starting in the most sensational way, with 18 for the first five holes, he accomplished the outward journey in 38 strokes—a performance which he even excelled coming homewards, and he finished, full of running, in 75, making his grand aggregate 314, or three better than Mr. Tait's. This brilliant effort completely altered the aspect of events, and all interest was now transferred to the doings of

Braid, who, with Pulford and A. Herd alone, had any chance of beating Mr. Hilton's total. When Mr. Hilton finished, Braid was at the "Rushes" hole, and hither, helter-skelter, sped Mr. Hilton's crowd, all agog with excitement. They learned that Braid's score to the 13th hole was 55, so that he only required to complete the remaining five holes in 22 strokes, or three under fives, to beat Mr. Hilton. Holing out in magnificent style at the "Field" hole in four, he still further improved his chance, and 18 to win, or 19 to tie, was now the comparatively easy task he had before him. The "Lake" hole he played steadily in five, leaving one five and two fours for the remaining three holes. But alas! the "Dun" hole proved disastrous to his chances. A raking tee shot, followed by a superb brassy, in which he crossed the corner of the field and lay about 30 yards short of the green, seemed to make a five certain. The approach to this green, however, is of the most tricky description, and Braid's ball, though beautifully struck, got a bad fall on the hard green, and shot past the hole, some 10 yards, into the rough ground beyond the green. He failed to get his long putt dead, and took six to hole out. Even yet, two fours would enable him to tie—

a three and a four seemed too much to hope for—but owing to weakness on the green at the 17th hole, he took five, so that even to tie with Mr. Hilton, he had to do the last hole in three. His second shot to the hole-side with his cleek was a beauty, and looked as if it were going to lie dead. It rolled some yards past, however, and as he failed to hole the long putt, he lost the championship by two strokes, finishing one stroke behind Mr. Hilton. Pulford and Herd, though again returning good scores of 79 and 80, had to be content with third and fourth places, Pulford tieing with Mr. Tait for third place. The final scores were as follows :—

	1st Day's Score.	2nd Day's Score.		
Mr. H. H. Hilton	155 ...	84	75 = 159	= 314
J. Braid	154 ...	82	79 = 161	= 315
Mr. F. G. Tait ...	158 ...	80	79 = 159	= 317
G. Pulford	159 ...	79	79 = 158	= 317
A. Herd	159 ...	79	80 = 159	= 318
H. Vardon	164 ...	80	76 = 156	= 320

As will be seen, H. Vardon, the holder, had the distinction of having the best aggregate on the second day of the competition, and though defeated on this occasion, he worthily upheld his reputation.

Mr. Hilton's win—his second in the open

championship—was warmly received, and there can be no question that his was a magnificent performance. The advantage of knowing the course as he does, no doubt counts for something, and though, in receiving the trophy, he modestly, in view of this fact, gave the greater merit to Braid, it seems probable that this advantage is much overestimated. A man may know a course too well. Mr. Hilton himself took 84 to his third round, and the fact that Braid returned a 74 in the competition, and H. Vardon a 76, is sufficient to show that, in the few days at their disposal, these players, at any rate, had managed to master a good deal of Hoylake's peculiarities.

Braid's play throughout was a treat to witness, and indeed more superb golf it would be difficult to conceive. He drives an exceedingly long and low ball, that keeps very straight, and the ball leaves the club as if shot from a cannon. His second stroke for the "Dun" hole in the final round, in which he successfully carried the corner of the field, straight on the hole, was, under the circumstances, a magnificent effort, and one that will live in the memory of all golfers who witnessed it.

Perhaps the most satisfying player to watch, however, was Mr. F. G. Tait. Mr. Tait's style is particularly fascinating, by reason of its quietness, and the suggestion it conveys of reserves of power. Here, there is nothing of the exuberant waggle of the professional, no wide straddle, or other strongly accented peculiarity. Nor is any trace of "side," temper, or playing to the gallery to be seen in Mr. Tait's play. His demeanour, playing before a crowd of 3,000, is like that of the soldier on parade. But after dinner, "Freddy," as he is known to his friends, can unbend, and whether blowing the bagpipes or proposing a toast, he takes, as he does at golf, a deal of beating.

Mr. Ryder Richardson, the club secretary, Mr. Harold Janion, and the rest of the club committee, did much to make the meeting one of the most successful gatherings of golfers that has ever been held.

CHAPTER X.

SANDWICH.

THE story of Sandwich, from the earliest historical period till the middle of the seventeenth century, is intimately bound up with the history and fortunes of England. In almost every event of historical importance that occurred, during all the centuries from the Roman occupation to the destruction of the Spanish Armada, Sandwich had a share, and bore an honourable part. From its exposed situation on the direct sea route to London from the south, its importance as a harbour, and its own wealth, it bore the brunt, through many centuries, of the successive Saxon and Scandinavian invasions, and when, after the Norman conquest, it became one of the chief Cinque Ports, it contributed in no small degree to the

SANDWICH.

(From a drawing by Gatsden G. Smith.)

consolidation of the kingdoms and the establishment of the naval supremacy of England.

Sandwich, in common with the other ports, had to provide ships and men at its own cost, for the King's service, for fifteen days or a longer period if their services were required. This fleet, which was the nucleus and germ of our present navy, and which in 1229 numbered fifty-seven ships, was spread proportionately over the five ports. It had its own ensigns and uniform, and its officers and men were persons of great consideration and importance. In return for their services, the ports enjoyed many immunities and privileges. They were self-governing corporations and their inhabitants were largely exempt from taxation. Their immunity from military service enabled them to give full play to their commercial instincts, and by their enterprise as sailors they created a large trade with the Continental nations, whose commerce they attracted by their wealth and the excellence of their harbours.

During all this long period, Sandwich, as has been said, was one of the most powerful and prosperous of the ports, and had its full share of honourable enterprise and glory. At the time of the Roman occupation, a broad estuary, called by the English, the Wantsum, and which reached from Sandwich to Reculver, separated the Isle of Thanet from the mainland, and though, after the departure of the Romans, this channel began to shrink, it remained for many hundreds of years part of the shortest sea route to London for all vessels coming from the south.

Standing as it did, at the southern end of this estuary, Sandwich became, as it were, the port of London. Its near proximity to the archiepiscopal city of Canterbury, and its situation as the first and last point of contact with the mainland for voyagers, to and from the Continent, the ecclesiastical capital, and London, gave it an importance difficult to conceive, in these days, when international communications have been indefinitely multiplied.

In course of time the Wantsum became gradually narrowed. The alluvial deposits which were brought into its basin by several rivers, ceased to escape seawards, owing to the blocking of their channels by the action of the tide on the sands, with the result that the sea was gradually shut out, and Thanet was restored to the mainland. The course of the Stour, however, remained open for many centuries, and Sandwich retained its maritime importance when others of the ports had fallen into decay.

But the shutting out of the tides, and the consequent blocking of the passage of the Stour seawards, hastened, if it did not create, the condition of things which is present to-day. The eastward drift of sand now proceeded unchecked, and, gradually encroaching on the bay on which Sandwich stood, drove the mouth of the river farther and farther northwards. At the present time it pursues a narrow and winding course of four miles, before it ultimately reaches the sea, and Sandwich has been left, high and dry, with some two miles of sandy waste between it and the sea which formerly washed its walls, and on which once rode proudly the navies of England.

But if the ancient glory and prosperity of Sandwich have long since departed; if its streets are now deserted and grass-grown, untrodden, as of yore, by the feet of dignitaries of Church and State; if Pegwell Bay, of old the landing-place of the invading Dane and Saxon, and where St. Augustine and his monks first set foot on our shores, is now given over to the peaceful shrimper and the cockney excursionist, Sandwich has experienced, in these latter years, a curious revival of prosperity.

An ancient adage runs—

> "Of many people it hath been sayed,
> That Tenterden steeple, Sandwich haven hath decayed."

And this puzzling statement is explained on the ground that funds that were set apart for the construction of a sea-wall were used for the building of the church. If the locking out of the sea and the consequent decay of Sandwich is thus to be laid at the door of the church, it should be remembered that to this clerical misappropriation of funds, and its consequences, Sandwich to-day owes its golf course and club, and the revival of trade and prosperity which have resulted therefrom.

History repeats itself, and what was sung by a northern poet, earlier in the century, of St. Andrews, may with equal force and appropriateness be said to-day of Sandwich :—

> "St. Andrews, they say that thy glories are gone,
> That thy streets are deserted, thy castles o'erthrown.
> If thy glories be gone, they are only methinks
> As it were by enchantment, transferred to thy links.
> Though thy streets be not now, as of yore, full of prelates,
> Of abbots and monks, and of hot-headed zealots,

Let none judge us harshly, or blame us as scoffers
When we say that instead, there are links full of golfers.
With more of good heart and good feeling among them
Than the abbots, the monks, and the zealots who sung them.
If golfers and caddies be not better neighbours,
Than abbots and soldiers, with crosses and sabres,
Let such fancies remain with the fool who so thinks,
While we toast old St. Andrews, its Golfers and Links."

Sandwich is now within three hours' railway journey of Cannon Street. A very good train leaves a little before 5 p.m. and lands the golfer at the Bell Hotel—a 'bus from which meets all trains—in time for dinner. It is a pleasant train to catch at any season of the year. With a good day's work well over, congenial society, and with three or four days of golf in prospect, he must be a hard man to please, who does not sit down to dinner, on his arrival, in a contented frame of mind.

No more delightful golfing holiday can be had near London. The "Bell" makes most comfortable headquarters, and the St. George's Club billiard, reading, and card-rooms, which have been added to the hotel, for the use of members and their friends, supply all needful after-dinner recreation. If the golfer has not the good fortune to be a member of the club, he will find, if his credentials are passable, that he will be treated with all courtesy and kindness by those who are members, in pleasing contrast to the treatment that is sometimes meted out to the passing stranger in other places. The hon. secretary is Mr. W. Rutherford.

A pleasant drive of a mile after breakfast, by a somewhat circuitous road, lands one at the club-house. In driving thither, one is struck by the absolutely Dutch-like colour and character of the landscape. The road passes through flat fields, chiefly devoted to market gardening, and intersected by straggling poplars. The usual English hedgerow is absent. Looking backward, the view of the quaint old town, with its windmill and two picturesque towers, is charming, and always, there is the delightful sensation of great, spreading skies and fresh air, which one gets with a low horizon.

The old farmhouse has been skilfully adapted to meet the club's requirements. With its huge encircling elms and glimpses of sloping thatch, no more picturesque club-house exists, and it has, besides, an air of comfort and prosperity, which is confirmed by subsequent experience of all the internal arrangements.

One great merit of Sandwich is, that it is never disagreeably crowded, except at meeting-times. The length and disposition of the holes, and the configuration of the ground is such, that it is possible, even with a good many players on the links, to play a whole round and not see a couple all the way.

There is Sunday golf, and what is equally important, there are Sunday caddies, and week-days or Sundays, under the management of Ramsay Hunter, these latter are a most civil and efficient body.

The golfer who takes his stand at the first tee, on the occasion of his first visit to Sandwich, without some searchings of heart and feelings of reverential awe, must have a proud and overweening spirit, and be sadly lacking in imagination and observation. It is quite certain, however, that one round of these magnificent links, will take the conceit, at least, out of all but the most case-hardened. All around is a wilderness of bent and broken hillocks, throughout which bunkers of portentous size and shape, gape with hungry maws, for errant balls. In the far distance, the "Maiden" raises her grisly brow, and seems to beckon derisively to the golfer, awaiting the moment, a few holes further on, when she can clasp him in her treacherous embrace. At his feet, to catch the primal "top" or "foozle," stretch 30 yards of morass. The hole seems far away, the course but narrow, and so bad is the country on either side, that the eye shrinks from contemplating it. The lip of a bunker can be descried guarding the hole. Nevertheless, with a stout heart, the green can be reached in two, unless the wind be strong against one. There is nothing amiss with a five for this hole, and he may deem himself lucky who gets a four.

The tee for the 2nd hole is to the right, and some 140 yards in front, stretches a very wide bunker, right across the course. A hill beyond, prevents the player from seeing the hole. Even if the wind be behind him, the safe line is to play over the right side of the bunker, where good lies and a view of the hole, over a second bunker, can be obtained. To the left of the bunker the ground is almost unplayable, and no advantage, practically, is gained by going straight, as there is extreme danger of reaching the second bunker. The second shot is an exceedingly difficult one. The green is on a sort of plateau, and unless the ball be struck on the exact line, it is almost certain to roll off the green, either to the right or left, and lie in a deep hollow below. This makes a very hard third stroke to play, and the player may congratulate himself if he holes in five, should his second stroke fail to stay on the green. Perhaps the best course is to play one's second strongly, beyond the hole, where the ground rises. This makes a certain five of it, and a possible four, if the putting comes off.

But now we are getting into the thick of things, and on the third tee, the stranger, gazing round in bewilderment, on a vast succession of most formidable bunkers, asks his caddie where the next hole can possibly be. A small direction flag is pointed out on an eminence, about 140 yards away, the road to which is one chaos of sand-holes and long bents, and nerving himself for the ordeal, and offering up a silent prayer, he prepares to strike. Here, again, a line on the right will be found to give the player a good lie, if he carry the hazards, but woe, unutterable woe, will be his portion, if he tops his tee shot. He will descend into the deep and wide abyss, armed with his niblick, and if he gets out in four, will be fortunate indeed. By carrying the ridge with his first, a wrist shot to the left, will land the ball on the green, and an easy four will be the result. With a strong following wind, long drivers occasionally play to carry over everything, straight on to the green from the tee, a distance of over 200 yards. Truly a Titanic shot!

The 4th hole is a longer one, and not to be reached in two, except by the longest drivers. The tee shot is over a considerable eminence faced by a large sand bunker. Once over this, a good lie is obtained, and a clean hit "brassy" should carry the player, over the intervening hollows and hillocks, to the neighbourhood of the green. This hole is a perfectly satisfactory five.

We are now on the confines of Deal, and here we turn to the left and play for the 5th hole, along a valley, in the direction of Pegwell Bay. If the wind be favourable, the green can be reached in one, but if, as often happens, it is right ahead, very wary steering is necessary. On the left, about 100 yards away, is a large and deep bunker, and on the right are two trappy pocket bunkers. Escaping these, however, the hole should be done in four without much trouble.

The "Maiden" is now looming close on our

left, and from this side, the formidable nature of the hazard is apparent, and claims our attention, for the next hole—the 6th—lies on its farther side. The "Maiden" is a huge sandhill, covered on the top with grass and bent, and on this near side it descends in a sheer precipice of sand, some 40 feet high, built up with piles and transverse beams to prevent the sand shifting, and terminating at its base in a wide expanse of stones and soft sand, honeycombed with footmarks. The opposing face of the bunker is so steep and high, and the standing and lies thereon so bad, that it is almost impossible, if a ball lies in it, to get it over, and the unhappy golfer has to thrash away at his ball, until such time as it rests in some more negotiable place. Playing back is no use, as there is no better ground within reach to play for, and the aggravating thing is, that the green can easily be reached with a mashie or cleek from the tee, when a three is quite obtainable.

The tee for the next, or 7th hole, is found in advance, and to the left of the "Maiden" putting green. It is a long hole, and presents no difficulty, if the initial bunker and a small "blind" pot over the bank, to the right, be avoided. There is plenty of elbow room, if one plays a little to the right.

By playing the second stroke short, and the third on to the green, this hole should be done in five, though, with an adverse wind, a six is not to be grumbled at.

The 8th hole—"Hades"—is an exceedingly pretty one. The green is guarded by a hill which looks like a small edition of the "Maiden." Unlike that hazard, however, it presents a smiling face to the player, and on the near side is grass grown and solid to the eye. But immediately over the ridge, "Hades" begins. The hazard is downhanging, terrible, and vast. Nevertheless a good cleek or mashie shot from the tee—unless against a head wind when nothing will be too much—will land the ball on one of the prettiest putting greens in the world, and result in a three, with the offchance of a two, to take the edge off possible future sevens or eights.

The next is the half-way hole, and is called the "Corsets," in allusion, doubtless, to the sinuous "switchback"-like outline of the woodwork, facing two long rows of parallel bunkers which confront one from the tee. A good swipe, over the left side of the first "Corset," will secure the player a good lie, and he will then be able, with an iron club, to carry the second and get on or near the green. This is a very tricky green to approach, and even with two good strokes to start with, the hole is much more often done in five than four.

Starting the homeward journey, the course for the 10th hole lies backward, parallel to the 9th, but on the lower ground, and the hole is near the green of "Hades." A good drive along the valley, followed by a long brassy or cleek according to the direction of the wind, will enable the player to carry a wide-spreading bunker and land his ball on the green. Like the last, this hole is a good four.

Turning seawards, the 11th hole is a drive, followed by an iron or cleek shot. The drive is over a bunker and some nasty hillocky country, abounding in bad lies and stands, and the second stroke has to be played over a ridge, but presents no special difficulty. This hole should be done in four.

The 12th hole is one of the most difficult in the whole round. If all goes well, it is a good five and an excellent four; but each stroke is so precarious, by reason of the abundance of hazards, that the golfer can never feel comfortable, until he sees his ball, actually at rest, on the putting green.

The tee shot is played over a ridge, running at an oblique angle across the player, and guarded, on the direct line, about 150 yards away, by a very catchy bunker. Should he carry this, or more safely, play over the ridge to the left, the player will obtain a view of the hole, and will probably have a good lie. But should he be short of the ridge, or to the right of it, he will be out of sight of the hole, and will most likely have a bad stand for his second stroke. His only safe course is then to play short, over the ridge to the left, with a view to getting on the green in three. The approach to the hole is guarded by a deep sandy road, with high banks, through which no ball can run, and just beyond the green are numerous pockets of sand and clumps of rushes, so that, unless the approach be played high and straight without much run on it, the ball is almost sure to land in grief.

For the 13th hole, the tee shot is played over the ridge down to the old racecourse. This is a long hole, and, like the 7th, presents no special difficulty, if the tee shot is played well over the ridge, where there is plenty of space and good ground. The hole should be played in five strokes.

The 14th is a long and difficult hole. Keeping straight, there is no trouble to be encountered from the tee, and this stroke should land the player's ball within 60 or 70 yards of the water jump. This is a nasty hazard, as it stretches across the whole width of the course, and is banked on the far side. Moreover, one frequently gets a hanging lie from the tee shot, and as it is still far from home, the tendency to press is here very hard to resist, with the result that the ball is often missed, and lands in the water. Getting well over in two, however, the green can be reached in the next stroke, with an iron, over a shallow but wide bunker which guards the green. With a wind against the player, the difficulty of this hole is enormously increased, and it is a great deal oftener done in seven than six. A five can only be registered by faultless play.

The next hole, the 15th, is another somewhat puzzling hole. The first bunker is not formidable, for it can easily be carried from the tee, and the course is here wide. But the green is guarded, at right angles, by a continuation of the same sandy road which guards the 9th hole, and which here presents the same impassable features. Two good swipes, with a favouring gale, will take one perilously near it, and as the hole is only a little way over the hazard, it makes a very nervous pitch for the iron or mashie. The putting green is very tricky, and the player has done well who holes in five.

There is another water jump at the 16th hole, set in winding fashion in a very rough country. With his tee shot, however, the player should carry this and reach the bank in front of the green, and with a well-judged approach should be down in four.

The 17th hole is cut at the bottom of a large hollow, in the shape of a "punch-bowl," from which the hole takes its name. There is a large trappy bunker to catch a feeble or slightly heeled drive from the tee, and there is bad ground on the left as well. The hole is guarded by a hill, and the second stroke must be played so as to run or loft well over this, or a four will not be easy of accomplishment.

At the last hole, having played a good tee shot, we again encounter our friend the sand road, or something very like him, guarding the green. A high straight second, not too strong, will put the player in the way of a comfortable four, and a very satisfactory conclusion to the round.

The praises of Sandwich have been said and sung many times, and Dr. Laidlaw Purves, who discovered its golfing possibilities, and those who were associated with him in making the green, deserve all praise for the enterprise and skill which they have manifested in laying out the present magnificent course. There is no nonsense or skittles about the golf at Sandwich. A man must be playing very fine golf indeed, to get round these eighteen holes in eighty-five strokes, even in the best of weather. A missed shot is always punished, usually summarily, and even if it escapes the ubiquitous hazard, the length of the holes makes recovery almost hopeless.

If a word of adverse criticism may be permitted, one might say, that perhaps too many of the shots are blind; and while it may be contended, with some force, that this lends a variety and interest to the play, which would be lacking in a more open disposition of the holes, still, for a championship course, this prevalent characteristic gives an undesirable advantage to players familiar with the proper and safe line, and accustomed to the holes in all states of the wind.

As compared with many other courses, moreover, there is a lack of opportunity, at many of the holes, for playing the shorter approach shots. Even when the green is guarded by a bunker, there is usually plenty of space to come and go on, and the delicate manipulation of wrist iron play is thus comparatively at a discount. The course, no doubt, has been designed, on more heroic lines, for long carries, both from the tee and from the second strokes, and for championship purposes, this, perhaps, is as it should be. The average golfer, however, who is no longer in the heyday of youthful vigour and energy, may be pardoned, if he thinks that the course would be improved, for ordinary play, by the shortening of several of the holes, so as to prevent the battle going, as it must do on the championship round, to the stronger, though not necessarily the more skilful, player.

The record of the green is held by Mr. C. E. Hambro, who returned a card of 78 in the competition for the St. George's Vase in 1897.

A stroll through the ancient town, after play, will well repay the golfer, though but little remains of the time when Sandwich was a flourishing seaport. A barge or two, a small coasting sloop or schooner, at the riverside, or making their tedious way towards the faithless sea, are the only

A BIT OF OLD SANDWICH.
(From a drawing by E. F. C. Clark)

suggestions of its former maritime glory. The ancient watergates and quays, the old wall, and all the picturesque paraphernalia of a fortified seaport, where they have not already disappeared, are fast tumbling into decay. The beautiful Norman tower of St. Clement's alone reminds one of the early times, and one or two old gates recall the grandeur of its mediæval history. For the rest, the houses, though they have been built in the winding streets, and upon the sites of older and grander dwellings, belong to a later and a decadent period, when money was scarcer, and the stream of commerce and travel, which had flowed for so many generations through its streets, was like its river, seeking other channels.

With the advent of golf, Sandwich has happily entered once more upon a career of prosperity. It will be strange indeed, as seems probable in the case, not only of Sandwich, but of others of the ports and ancient towns, if the very causes which led to their decay, after the zenith of their greatness had been reached, should be the means, in a more peaceful age, of restoring to them something of their ancient prosperity.

CHAPTER XI.

CONCERNING STYLE.

PEOPLE who are ignorant of golf, and whose first introduction to the game is to watch a match between two first-class players, usually get the idea, that the accurate hitting of a golf ball is a very simple matter. There seems to be no difficulty about it. The player walks smartly up to his ball, gives a little careless flourish of his club, swings it rapidly backward, and crack! away goes the ball some 150 yards through the air! These same people betray no enthusiasm or appreciation at a quarter shot laid dead, or at the holing of a long putt, and even exhibit some disappointment, that the skill of the players falls so far short of holing out full strokes!

Half an hour with a driver and a golf ball, however, will go a long way towards opening such people's eyes to the realities of the situation. The truth is, that to hit a golf ball accurately, is one of the most difficult and delicate operations in the world, and demands for its successful execution the very nicest adjustment of all the complicated machinery which it calls into play. For consider for a moment the conditions.

First of all the golf club is not a weapon of precision. Its long and tapered shaft, its small head, so far away from the player's eye, with its still more restricted hitting surface, cannot fail to suggest, so soon as it is handled, that it is but indifferently adapted for its purpose. Then the small size of the ball, still further reduced by the nature of the ground from which it has to be struck, and the fact that considerable force must be applied, are all matters that must fill the beginner's mind with doubts and fears. As he proceeds he will find, in addition, that not only must he strike the ball, wherever it lies, on one particular part of its circumference, but that this must be done with a very particular part indeed of the club face, held at an equally particular angle, and that unless these two points are brought thus accurately, in contact, failure will be the result.

It is to the realisation of these painful facts, and the attempts of uninstructed and unobservant beginners to combat them, that our golf links are cumbered, as they are, with golfers exhibiting such perplexing varieties of style. Those weird and monstrous contortions, which so many a golfer's body goes through, in the act of striking, are but the combined result of the painful efforts of earnest but misguided men to adapt the cumbrous machinery to its work, of their consciousness that the instrument is very ill adapted for its purpose, and of their belief in the necessity for compensating, in some way, its unhandiness.

But it is not thus, in fear and ignorance, out of attempts to counteract the length and spring of your golf club, and to defeat the operations of natural law by the convulsions and contractions of your body, that success will emerge. There is a right way to use a golf club. There is a possibility of so handling and swinging the club, that it ceases to feel an awkward encumbrance and becomes as it were part of the golfer's frame, like an added member, which will work, if he be in form, in obedience to his will, as easily and certainly as his hand.

It is to the acquiring of this consistent and

harmonious *rapprochement* between club, hand, and eye that a golfer's style should be built up. One is pretty safe to say that no man ever acquired a good golfing style, who had not had many opportunities of seeing and playing with first-class players. In golf, as in other fine arts, proficiency is only to be attained, by intimate knowledge and study of the best masters. Mere slavish copying of the mannerisms of any one is of course useless, but it is only by close observation of the methods of good players, that one gets an insight to the broad underlying principles, and arrives at the proper golfing attitude of mind. Here, as in the other arts, all the great masters exhibit wide divergencies in the matter of style, and it is impossible, where all are good, to say definitely, that any one style is better than another. It is a matter of taste and opinion. The learner will observe, however, that these divergencies in the styles of good golfers, are merely the natural and proper result of individual idiosyncracies of physique and temperament, and not of any essential difference in the force and accuracy with which they hit the ball. He will be wise then who, in endeavouring to acquire a good style of golf, concerns himself with observing where the styles of good players are in agreement, and who pays no attention to the minor details where they differ. If the root of the matter is in him, his golfing instincts will soon find for themselves adequate and appropriate expression, and may be safely left to take care of themselves.

Yet though it may be difficult, and even impossible, to determine what are the good points in a style of golf, there are certain faults and vices of style, about which it is possible to arrive at a more definite finding, inasmuch as they are never found in the styles of good players, and against these errors the beginner must be on his guard.

It is difficult to understand how such a heresy as "slow-back" was ever seriously entertained and put forward as a nostrum for golfers, opposed, as it is, to all the teachings of experience and the practice of the best performers. If there is one point which strikes the observer more than another, in watching the play of good golfers, it is the decision and rapidity of all their movements. Neither in addressing the ball, nor in the backward or forward swing, is there ever anything of slowness or undue deliberation. The backward and the forward swing are parts of one and the same movement, and should be as harmonious and continuous as possible, and so long as the club is brought forward faster on the ball than it went up, and the balance is preserved, there is not much danger that the club will be swung backwards too rapidly.

The "waggle" or preliminary flourish of the club over the ball, the object of which is the freeing of the wrists and arms, and of ensuring that the club lies properly in the hands, has come to be, if indeed it has not always been, an indispensable adjunct of the good golfer's style. If a man has no "waggle," you may be sure that his play will be lifeless and poor. The "waggles" of good players vary, like the other details of their play, but they all agree in two points—they are never unduly prolonged, and they are usually rather quick and nervous movements. After the completion of the waggle, it is the invariable practice to rest the club-head on the ground, for an instant, before swinging, close behind the ball, in the exact position and at the exact angle, in which the player desires it to return on the ball. This indeed is done at the commencement of the waggle, and may be done also during its progress, for the purpose of enabling the player to find his proper distance from the ball, but it is essential that it should be thus grounded, just before striking. Some players have a habit, when they ground the club, of placing either its toe or its heel opposite the ball, but to do either of these things is to court failure. If either eccentricity be indulged in, or if the club be grounded altogether clear of the ball, the difficulty of the stroke is increased tenfold, as the player starts his swing from a false point, and has to correct his aim during the process of swinging, with obvious diminution both of force and accuracy.

It is hardly possible to define accurately, what constitutes a correct golfing swing, and, as before indicated, the only thing that can usefully be done, is to observe the points where the swings of good players agree, and to note where they differ from those of inferior performers. The first thing that can safely be affirmed about the true golfing stroke is, that in its essential nature, it is a swing, and not a hit. This hitting with rigid arms and wrists, which one sees so much of in England, is cricket, and not golf, and although, with a good eye, a man may bump the ball along in this fashion, it is a style that will never lead to excellence, and it is against all the spirit and traditions of the game. The distance which the club is swung backwards is immaterial, provided that it is not taken so far back that the balance is lost, and force is expended uselessly in recovering it. A backward swing that is too short, is apt to be jerky and wanting in power, and it will be found that the swings of the best players are of medium length.

The true golf swing is always of a circular nature, and the club-head should always pursue the same orbit, in its downward course, that it does in its upward, whether the elliptical curve it describes, be of a high or perpendicular nature, or a flatter and more horizontal one.

Another point common to the swings, be they long or short, of all good players, is what is known technically as the "follow through." This characteristic marks them off definitely from all the hitting styles of golf, in which the club-head is practically arrested at the moment of contact with the ball. In the correct golf swing, both force and direction are imparted by this following through. The ball is regarded merely as a point *through* which the club-head passes in its course, and at the instant when it has attained its greatest momentum. After sweeping away the ball, the club-head passes onwards and gradually upwards, the weight of the arms and body, following the direction of the stroke, being thrown, as it were, after the ball, and the player, at the end of the stroke, is facing the line of the ball's flight, the club going up over the left shoulder.

It is not here contended that the club continues to control the flight of the ball, *after* striking it. Whatever the nature of the swing may be, the ball leaves the club-head at the very instant of impact, and for good or ill the latter has no further effect on its course. The "follow through," however, is an essential characteristic of a good swing, as only where it is present can the maximum of force and direction be attained.

Another prevailing characteristic of a good swing is that there is no waste of energy. Every scrap of force that is used, is expended to advantage, in the right way, and at the right time. There are players, and good players, who, by reason of strength or superabundance of energy, seem to load their swings with sundry excrescences of ornament or action; but if they are good players, it will be found that the swing comes through at the finish, clean and true, and with no loss of force or intention.

It is a common vice with players, to sway the body to the right, at the commencement of the swing, which, of course, throws them off their balance at once. The balance of the body should be preserved, and its weight, as it were, gradually accumulated, until the very finish of the swing. Equally fatal is the vice of pulling the hands away backwards, in advance of the club-head, for this throws the swing out of gear at its commencement. The club should be swept backwards, evenly and without jerk, the player's head must be kept steady, and the eye firmly fixed on the part of the ball that he desires to strike.

Though these remarks have been made in reference to full strokes, subject to certain obvious modifications, they may be taken as applying equally to all golfing strokes. As a matter of style, a golfer should endeavour to make all his strokes, in regard to grip, stance, and swing, as far as it may be possible, in the same manner. Nothing looks worse than to see a player, who stands erect over his full strokes, crouching down to play an approach or putt, and nothing is more fatal to accuracy, than the practice of playing full shots off the left leg, and quarter shots off the right. As far as the nature of the ground and the length of the club will permit, he should always endeavour to take up the same stance, for each stroke.

All these things, however, are general principles outside which, as has been said, it is not safe or useful to dogmatise in discussing style. So much depends, even after a player is thoroughly well grounded in the correct theory of the golfing stroke, upon accidents of physique and temperament. In this matter of style, as in all other parts of the game, the golfer will infallibly reveal something of his inner character. The quiet and reserved nature will manifest itself in the simplicity and directness of its methods; the fussy man will fuss and fidget over his strokes, as he does in the ordinary affairs of the world.

There is still one aspect of style in golf, about which it may be possible to say something. We refer to its æsthetic aspect. Granted, that if results are good, the style must be good, it is still possible that, like the Scotch girl, it may be good without being "bonny"; and, though tastes and opinions may differ as to the relative merits of various styles, there are general principles of beauty, universally accepted and admitted, which may safely be applied, to the partial settling of the matter.

One of the first essentials which a thing must possess, if it is to be called beautiful, as distinct from good, is, that the means which are employed in producing it are adequate. They must show no sign, on the one hand, of insufficiency, nor on the other, of superfluity. The best artistic result is obtained, and the highest æsthetic impression conveyed, when there is an exact ratio between the means and the result. If this law be applied to the styles and strokes of good players, very few indeed will be found to come within the category of the beautiful. Excellent results are common, but they are too often attained by the violation of this law of the needful and the adequate. Exaggerations of stance and attitude, exuberance of waggle, undue rigidity of body or unseemly suppleness, mar the styles of many a good player, and put them outside the pale of the æsthetic.

Another accepted test of the beautiful is, that in its expression, it should give evidence of reserve. A fine stroke at golf, like a fine work of art, should always leave the impression, if it is to be altogether pleasing, that it has been produced without struggle, that its originator has not had to strain himself in order to do it, and that he has plenty of reserves of strength and skill left behind, for subsequent masterpieces.

Judged by this standard again, how many excellent golfers must fail!

Amongst living players, taken in conjunction with their magnificent play, the styles of Mr. John Ball, jun., Mr. F. G. Tait, Mr. H. G. Hutchinson, and Willie Fernie seem most nearly to approach the ideal. All four styles at least justify the appellation "pretty," and all are graceful and full of reserve. The powerful style of Willie Park, jun., possesses great elements of beauty, but it seems marred by a slight skewness of the upward swing, which suggests doubts as to the ultimate direction in which the ball will go.

The styles of Taylor, the Vardons, Braid, and a score of other fine players, amateur and professional, have all excellent points of execution, but fall short of the æsthetic qualities of the five above named. We have our golfing Titians, like Blackwell and Rolland; our Holbeins, like Herd, Kirkaldy, and Balfour-Melville; and our little

Dutch Masters, like Hilton and Bernard Sayers, but all more or less labouring, like their prototypes, and winning their bread by the sweat of their brows. The Velasquez of golf has not yet arisen.

CHAPTER XII.

LONDON GOLF.

TEN years ago there were not half a dozen golf clubs within hail of the Metropolis. To-day, within a radius of twelve miles of the chief railway stations, there are nearly fifty. When it is considered that these clubs have an average membership of 200, and that, apparently, they are all in a growing and flourishing condition, some idea may be gathered of the rapid and sure hold that golf has taken on the affections of the London public. If further proof is needed of the vitality of London golf, a tour round the various greens will convince the most sceptical, of the extent and reality of the movement. Most of the golf clubs in the immediate neighbourhood of London, have been instituted in the teeth of enormous difficulties. To say nothing of the huge rent that has to be paid for a suitable piece of land, the ground itself, in many cases, is of such a nature, that only the most determined and enthusiastic spirits would have dared to think of it in connection with golf; for a great part of London and its neighbourhood lies upon a bed of clay. To the south and south-west, and also in some of the eastern districts, where the channels of rivers are to be found, or where they have formerly existed, there are large deposits of gravel, but in the north and north-west, gravel regions are few and far between. For golfing purposes, London clay is probably about the worst form of soil in the world. It produces, with extreme rapidity, in the growing months, a coarse and rank kind of grass, and as, in wet weather, the ground becomes exceedingly soft and sloppy, the grass, if walked upon, gets trodden down into the clay, and old and close turf seldom gets a chance to grow. In dry weather, the clay becomes as hard as concrete, and it is only when the ground is between these two extremes, that the game can be played, with anything like an approach to the proper conditions.

In addition, it is almost impossible to drain London clay. It holds the water in a way that no other soil does, while the expense of keeping the grass down is enormous. Then there are trees and tall hedges, and, worse than all, multitudinous worm casts, which are the despair of the green-keeper, and render the making and maintaining of good putting greens an impossibility. Nevertheless, golf is played and enjoyed by hundreds of players, every day, in the vicinity of London ; and on many courses where the subsoil is gravel, the golf is as good as can be found anywhere, away from the seashore.

The Royal Blackheath Club, as it is the oldest established golf club in the world, merits the first place in any notice of London clubs. It was founded in 1608, no doubt by the Scottish Court during its residence at Greenwich. The links are situated within the Metropolitan area, seven miles from Victoria or Ludgate Hill, and the nearest stations to the heath are Greenwich or Blackheath Hill. The course consists of seven holes, and for purposes of matches and medals, it is played three times round. The holes are of great length, the 4th and 5th, which, with the others, have to be played three times in the course of a round, measure respectively 550 and 520 yards. The subsoil is gravel, with a large admixture of flints and pebbles, which play havoc with one's irons. There are but few hazards of the orthodox kind, although a few stunted whins may remind one that, in the old times, the face of the heath had a somewhat different aspect. There is an old gravel pit, called "Marr's Ravine," which is the most formidable hazard, and sundry other hollows and plateaus make the play to some of the holes more or less interesting.

But on the whole Blackheath is a sad place. Its glory has departed. Surrounded on all sides by the smug Victorian residences of the retired middle classes, intersected by roads garnished with lamp-posts and railings, with nursemaids, and perambulators, and infants' schools, swarming on the green, a game of golf on Blackheath is now a curious experience. Even the club-house —filled with priceless golfing relics of the past— which not so very long ago was on the heath, has been overwhelmed by the advancing tide of brick and mortar, and now occupies a humble and retired situation in a back street.

What the increase of population and the consequent increase of building have failed to accomplish, in the way of spoiling the beauties and amenities of the old heath, the County

Council, who now control it, are rapidly finishing. "Glennie's Hole," "Sleepy Hollow," and other historic hazards and features have been improved away, and the place is now almost as beautiful and diversified as a bleach-green. Only the other day the writer noticed a gang of workmen at work in "Marr's Ravine."

In spite of all this, the Royal Blackheath Club goes on its way courageously, and plays for its ancient trophies with unfailing regularity. Mr. F. S. Ireland and Mr. J. G. Gibson, two ex-captains, fully maintain the reputation of Blackheath golfers. The onerous duties of hon. secretary and hon. treasurer, are ably discharged by ex-captain W. G. Barnes and Mr. J. S. Sawyer respectively, and the members, generally, are keenly alive to the preservation of all the ancient rites and customs of the club.

Next in order of seniority and importance, in the roll of London links, must come Wimbledon. The common is the home green of two golf clubs — viz., the London Scottish Golf Club, formed in 1865, and the Royal Wimbledon Golf Club, which is an offshoot of the other, founded in the same year. The London Scottish club-house is at the north end of the common, and that of the Royal Wimbledon at the south. If the player be the guest of the former, Putney is his nearest station, which can be reached either from Waterloo or Ludgate Hill. If the Royal Wimbledon Club be his hosts, then he must take his ticket to Wimbledon, from Waterloo or Victoria. Both clubs play over the same ground, but the London Scottish start their round from the north end, and the Royal Wimbledon from the south.

The common is now under the control of "Conservators," and golf is only permitted on Tuesdays, Thursdays, and Saturdays. The course is, without doubt, one of the best near London. There are bad lies to be had, and there is much stony ground, and many balls may be lost in the all-pervading whins, but the hazards are natural, and the holes are of the most sporting character and of excellent lengths. The putting greens are beautiful, and of the proper undulating nature.

As the common stands high, the air is healthful and bracing, and lovely views are obtained of the plains and hills of Surrey, with foregrounds of whins and heather, or waving birch.

The Royal Wimbledon Club have been fortunate in securing the services of J. H. Taylor as resident professional and club-maker, while another good player, Peter Fernie, acts in the same capacities, for the London Scottish.

In 1872, a ladies' golf course was laid out at Wimbledon, and a very pretty little course it is. The Wimbledon Ladies' Golf Club was the first recognised ladies' club, and to Wimbledon, therefore, belongs the credit of initiating a movement that is now far-spread and popular.

Many fine players belong to the Wimbledon clubs. The names of A. H. Molesworth, T. R. Pinkerton, W. Laidlaw Purves, and Norman R Foster, the latter the hon. secretary and treasurer of the Royal Wimbledon Club, are familiar to all golfers. The secretary of the London Scottish is Mr. James Gow.

Richmond, not far off, which can be reached from Waterloo or Mansion House, can boast two excellent courses. The course of the Mid-Surrey Golf Club, situated in the Old Deer Park, is close to the station. It is one of the driest near London, the soil being gravel and sand; and though the ground is flat, the eighteen holes are of good length, and have been well, if somewhat monotonously, guarded with artificial bunkers.

The putting greens are large and good, and the going throughout the course, unless one be very much off the line, is excellent. There is a large and well-appointed club-house. The club, though of recent origin, numbers some good players among its members, among whom Mr. S. H. Fry, the amateur billiard champion, is pre-eminent, not only for the actual brilliancy of his play, but for the rapidity with which he achieved excellence.

A drive of fifteen minutes from Richmond station, takes the golfer to Sudbrooke Park, the headquarters of the Richmond Golf Club. This course is, in some respects, superior to any other near London. A splendid subsoil of yellow sand rendered the making of artificial bunkers easy, and these have been most judiciously constructed and placed. There are eighteen holes of various lengths, and natural hazards in the shape of ponds, ditches, &c., abound. But the great glory of Sudbrooke Park is its putting greens, the turf on them is beautifully close and even, and of unvarying quality.

The weak point of the course is the number of trees, many of which greatly interfere with the play. A great deal has been done in the way of removing the more obviously impossible ones, but there are still many that baulk or catch a good stroke. Mr. John Gairdner, under whose able captaincy the course was greatly improved, is in the first flight of amateur players.

The ground of Prince's Golf Club is at Mitcham, close to Mitcham Junction station, and can be reached from Victoria in about twenty minutes. The course is a common, and the subsoil being gravel, it is dry. The eighteen holes are of great length, and the lies throughout the green are rapidly improving. The record of the green is 76—a truly fine score made by Mr. Ernley Blackwell, the bogey score being 84. There is an excellent ladies' golf course of eighteen holes. The resident professional is that well-known player, Jack White, late of North Berwick.

Not far away, at Furzedown, is the links of the Tooting Bec Golf Club, the station for which is Tooting Junction, which can be reached either from Victoria or London Bridge. One of the first to establish a private golf links near London, the Tooting Bec Club is now one of the most prosperous clubs in the neighbourhood of the Metropolis. The Parliamentary Golf Handicap competition takes place annually over the course, and the club numbers in its ranks many men, distinguished, not only in the golfing world, but in all departments of human activity. The course is undulating, with plenty of natural and artificial hazards. The soil is gravel, and the lies throughout the green and the putting greens are excellent. The members are happy in the possession of a commodious and comfortable club-house, and in Peter Paxton, as resident professional, they have an experienced club-maker and an efficient coach. The record score for the green is 74.

Eight miles from London Bridge is another influential club, the Eltham Golf Club, instituted in 1892. Though the clayey nature of the soil is against a uniform excellence being maintained throughout the year, the club have been able, by judicious draining and constant attention, to get the course into good condition. The names of Mr. Arnold Blyth, Mr. A. S. Johnston, Mr. R. H. Hedderwick, and Mr. John Penn, M.P., on the list of members, are sufficient proof both of the golfing prowess of its members, and of the ability with which the affairs of the club are managed.

The park is most picturesquely situated, and the club-house, which is the ancient Manor Lodge, is one of the most palatial in the kingdom. The bogey score is 80, but the record for the course is 70, a score which was compiled by W. Toogood, the club's professional.

"Down east," from Liverpool Street are more well-known clubs. The Royal Epping Forest Club play at Chingford, eleven miles from Liverpool Street station. The course is laid out on the waste land of Epping Forest, and though picturesque in situation and aspect, it suffers in wet weather from the clayey nature of the soil. The club rooms are attached to the Royal Forest Hotel, which is only about five minutes' walk from Chingford Station. Without having any players of outstanding merit, the Royal Epping Forest Club can put a strong match team in the field. There is no Sunday play.

Further out, some forty minutes from town, is the picturesque and excellent new course of the Romford Golf Club. It is of great extent, and great pains have been taken to lay the holes out to the best advantage, so as to avoid crossing, and to make use of all the natural features. Owing to its flatness, the holes are somewhat monotonous in character. James Braid, than whom no finer golfer exists, is the club professional. There is a comfortable club-house with one or two bedrooms, and Sunday play is permitted.

There is no Sunday play at Wanstead Park, nearer town—the station for which is Snaresbrook, also on the Great Eastern Railway—which is a pity, for a better course does not exist in this locality, so near London. The holes are of good length and of a very sporting character, and the subsoil is gravel. The hazards and greens are natural and of an excellent golfing quality.

Coming into town again, and starting from Paddington by the Great Western Railway, there is the green of the West Middlesex Golf Club, at Hanwell. This is a first-rate sporting little course of 18 holes, with fine putting greens. The soil varies, however, from sand and gravel to the ordinary clay of London, but in ordinary weather it is a charming course.

Ten minutes further by train is the golf course of the West Drayton Golf Club—the club-house, the picturesque old Mill House—being close to the station. This is another good 18-hole course, and a sound test of golf. It is dry and devoid of trees, and the turf is of first-rate and uniform quality. The club have had the advantage of the experience and advice of Mr. F. A. Fairlie, the well-known player, one of the members, in laying out the course, and this has been so well done, that the green must rank as one of the best near London. The river Brent wanders picturesquely through the course, and forms an awkward hazard at some of the holes. As the club is close to the station, the West Drayton Golf Club is one of the most convenient in the neighbourhood of London.

At Cassiobury Park, near Watford, the West Herts Club are now installed in a course that will be hard to beat near London; and nearer Euston, a mile or two from Harrow, from which station there runs a branch line, is the fine course of the Stanmore Golf Club. A hill of wide extent and gently sloping, is a great feature of Stanmore, and from the 3rd, 4th, and 9th holes, magnificent views of the surrounding country are commanded. The Stanmore Club are fortunate in having had as their captain, Mr. J. A. Begbie, who bears a name well known in golfing circles in Scotland, and who has done much to bring the club into its present flourishing condition.

On the St. John's Wood Railway, from Baker Street, the Northwood Golf Club have a fine 9-hole course, near the station of the same name. At Wembley Park, Mr. A. E. Stoddart, the well-known cricketer, has fallen a victim to golf, and, as report says, is making astonishing progress at the game, over this prettily situated course. Still nearer London, at Neasden, the Neasden Golf Club, with an unrivalled situation and a charming club-house, are struggling, through the winter months, with the problem of London clay. In the spring and summer no more delightful and sporting course exists.

Elsewhere at Finchley, at Muswell Hill, Enfield, Woodford, Epsom, Woking, Chiswick, and many other places, golf is to be had, of varying excellence, according to the nature of the soil.

On the whole, one can safely regard the golfing ground near London with a sort of chastened appreciation.

Like the curate with his bad egg, we can at least protest, when its quality is questioned, that "parts of it are excellent," and it may safely be affirmed, and I say it in no carping or cynical spirit, but simply as stating the fact, that it is probably as good as the golf played on it. When he thinks of the vast army of beginners who have ploughed their way to comparative efficiency through the mud-heaps of Metropolitan golf, a sense of gratitude must steal over the golfer's soul. He will inevitably reflect, that every wound inflicted on the groaning ground, every divot and skelp carved from the bowels of London links, is one saved from the already overworked greens by the sea-shore. And when the "agriculturalist" returns in summer, the seaside links can at least greet him with a whole skin, and his weapon's edge cannot fail to have lost something of its cruelty and keenness. By the stripes of the links of London are the others healed.

If one were to measure the excellence of Metropolitan golf greens, by the health and enjoyment they afford to thousands of overworked and over-idle men, it would be impossible to overestimate their value. They are sanatoriums for the mind and body, which give the city dweller glimpses of the quiet country, and enable him to forget, for an hour or two, the struggle and turmoil of city life.

CHAPTER XIII.

GOLFING ETIQUETTE.

ONE would think that most of the ten provisions contained in the "Etiquette of Golf," which are to be found at the end of the St. Andrews Rules, are so obvious, that it is a work of supererogation to print them. The exercise of common sense, and the display of a little consideration for other people, one might imagine, would be sufficient to solve any difficulty that might arise, and guide the golfer to his proper behaviour in course of play. But in actual experience, we find that things are far otherwise. On the links, common sense and consideration for other people, are two qualities that are seldom met with. The golfer is a selfish animal, and so long as he gets his own game, he is too often quite careless how he obstructs or spoils other people's enjoyment by his procedure.

In many places, the golf links are reached from the nearest town by a short railway journey, and the players from town all come by a certain train. Now, it is the invariable practice, at all such places, for the resident golfers to assemble on the first tee, just before this train comes in. They, of course, have to get off first, and the result, for the visitors, is a wait of varying duration on the first tee, blocked greens, and spoiled tempers all day. If these residents would only start a quarter of an hour earlier, all this loss of time and temper would be avoided.

Clause No. 1 of the Etiquette of Golf runs: "No player, caddie, or onlooker should move or talk during a stroke." To this it is necessary to add, that the proper place for all onlookers, is either behind the player's back, at a safe distance, or directly opposite him as he addresses the ball. Many people have a habit of standing behind the line of fire, in such a position that they catch the eye of the player in the process of striking.

Clause No. 3 says that: "The player who leads from the tee should be allowed to play before his opponent tees his ball."

The object of this is, that the first player may not be hampered in his choice of tee, or obstructed in his stroke, by his opponent or his caddie, and, for these ends, it is well for the opponent and his caddie to keep off the teeing ground altogether, unless it be very large, until his partner has teed and played off.

The regulations as to parties passing each other are quite clear and definite, and yet, in the application of them, many golfers are incorrigibly stupid and inconsiderate.

It is the commonest thing for a match, looking for a lost ball, to make no sign to the party coming up to pass them, even though they may have been looking for their ball some minutes. If they do call them on, as it is their duty to do, and should they immediately thereafter find their ball, it quite frequently happens that they proceed to play, as if the party passing were not in existence. If the ball be found, after consent to pass has been given, the consenting party must not play, until the match passing has holed out and moved away.

In the case of a three-ball match, or a party playing a shorter round, it is equally the duty of these, to give the match following, the opportunity to pass, if they wish, and should they accept, they must wait on the next tee, until the others have left it and are out of range.

A player playing by himself has no status, and must allow all matches to pass him, if desired. The plea which I once heard such a player advance, that he was not playing by himself, but against "Colonel Bogey," though ingenious, cannot be sustained.

Many golfers have a habit, when their opponents have a shortish putt for the hole, of walking away from the green, before he has holed the ball. The result very often is, that the player, thinking that the hole has been given up, is careless or hurried, and often misses the putt, whereupon the half is claimed by the opponent. The proper course to adopt with a player who behaves in this manner, is to follow him to the tee without holing. This trick is akin to that of the billiard player, who when his opponent, in play, is 97 or 98, and has a comparatively easy shot to win, puts his cue in the rack, with an ostentatious rattle. The player should claim the game without playing the stroke.

There is one kind of golfer who meets with universal execration, and the more so as his particular idiosyncracies seem to be beyond the reach of cure. I refer to the slow man.

The man who fusses about choosing a tee, and aims about a minute at his ball before striking it; who stares after it long after it has ceased to move, and walks at a snail's pace to where it lies, only to go through the same performance, regardless of a crowded green, richly deserves the anathemas which are always showered upon him. This slowness, which so many golfers suffer from, is the more irritating to the beholder, as it is always accompanied by bad play and is, indeed, fatal to excellence. No good player ever plays slow. Watch any match between two good players. They lose no time in choosing their tees, and the balls once teed, are despatched on their ways, in the twinkling of an eye, and the players move after them before the last has ceased to roll.

There is a class of golfer about whom it seems necessary to say a word, when dealing with the question of golfing etiquette and behaviour. I refer to the "pot-hunter."

For the man who is constantly playing for prizes, who runs about all over the country, wherever there is a handicap competition for cruet-stands or clocks, or who belongs to one or two London golf clubs, and plays, as some have been known to do, for two or three different prizes, at different greens, in one day, no word of condemnation is strong enough, for, in his case, he cannot be playing for the enjoyment of the game. But it has become the fashion to apply this opprobrious epithet to any golfer, who wins one or two prizes, and thus establishes his position as a good player, and it is this unfair use of the word that it seems necessary to combat. In the mouths of many, and these, be it remarked, are usually the unsuccessful competitors in the same competition, the winner is immediately a "pot-hunter"! According to these gentlemen, it is the crime of being a successful golfer that makes a man a "pot-hunter." So long as, like themselves, he only "hunts" unsuccessfully, they graciously allow him to retain his status as a fair and gentlemanly player. A palpable exhibition of envy, malice, and all uncharitableness such as this would be ludicrous, were it not so common, but those to whom the sportsmanlike traditions of the game are dear, may well ask whether, in view of its existence, it would not be desirable to curtail the number of prize competitions which so many clubs now indulge in.

The desire to excel, and the ambition to be first are natural and laudable feelings, in sport, as in all the other walks of life, and it is well and seemly that the conqueror should bear away with him some token of his victory. But the laurel wreath, which crowned the Isthmian winner, was surely in better taste than the machine-made coffee-pot or egg-boiler, which is the common reward of our sporting heroes to-day. Why donors of prizes should fly, as they invariably do, to the cheap jeweller and the Brummagem dealer, and spend their money on hideous, and for the most part, useless, specimens of their wares, when for the same money they could purchase artistic and beautiful things, is a deep mystery. Are there no artists left in the world, to design and fashion beautiful and appropriate trophies, as the reward of victory, which a man may buy, or win, and not be ashamed?

The question of what one ought to wear, or what ought not to be worn, in playing golf, is beset with extreme difficulty. Most good players, it may be observed, study comfort and utility in their apparel, rather than elegance; but it is possible to carry both these guiding principles to extremes, and a ludicrous contrast is sometimes presented by the spectacle of these two types, engaged in a match. The one, in an old shooting-coat, baggy trousers and shapeless boots, the other, resplendent in scarlet coat with brass buttons, riding breeches and white gaiters, and both equally intent on the game. There seems no good reason, however, why a man should not be well dressed at golf, but be he well or ill-dressed, he will in this matter, as in his play, inevitably reveal something of his nature. The pattern of his stockings, or the colour of his tie, are infallible guides to his æsthetic standpoint. Let the golfer, then, who is not sure of his instinct in such matters, turn a deaf ear to the blandishments of his outfitter, and provide himself with useful and unostentatious articles of apparel. He may wear a red coat without offence, remembering, however, that it is not an emblem of golfing eminence, but only a danger signal to the passer-by; but let him eschew flannels, and tennis shoes, and the baring of arms, for these things are an abomination, being utterly unnecessary, and opposed to the stern traditions of the game.

What would be said of a cricketer who turned up at Lord's in knickerbockers and hob-nailed boots? Men should remember that golf is quite as ancient and serious a game as cricket, and that its traditions are at least equally dear to its votaries, and worthy of respect.

It is a good plan, when it is your honour, and you have struck your own ball from the tee, not to run after it immediately, before your opponent has played his. By attending to this point, you will not endanger any good opinion he may have conceived of you, and you will escape the imminent risk of being killed by his ball.

When playing against a player whose handicap is considerably less than your own, do not, if you think you are not playing up to your true form and miss short putts, keep saying to him, "Well, I ought to have won that hole from you." Or, if off your driving or quarter game, "I can't understand how it is, I can't hit a single ball to-day." If you persist in this line of remark, you will most probably provoke your opponent to retort, that if you are in the way of holing all your putts and hitting every ball clean, what the deuce is he giving you strokes for!

It is of no use getting irritated with the opponent, whose only comments on the game in progress, are remarks drawing attention to the marvellous luck that you enjoy, in contrast to the bad luck that invariably pursues him. A genial acquiescence, in the one case, and cordial sympathy, in the other, will have an admirable effect in preserving your own game and temper, and, at the same time, will probably suggest to your opponent, as the game goes on, and if he has any sense of humour, the absurdity of his conduct. This habit of blaming luck at golf for one's mistakes, breeds in many golfers the most diverting absurdities. The player who exclaimed "Cupped again!" when he topped his tee shot, is a good instance of the disastrous effects of this habit of mind. There are others who, if they cannot by any stretch of imagination set down their bad play to bad luck, will invent all manner of other excuses for it. A good story is told of a St. Andrews player, who, having missed a putt, in dead silence, within a foot of the hole, immediately remarked, "Ah, somebody must have moved."

But absurd and annoying as are the vagaries of the "luckless," there is another class of golfer whose proceedings are even more trying to his partner or opponent. There is "the man with a temper." The "luckless" is usually a fatalist and suffers more or less meekly, or at worst peevishly, the stings and arrows of outrageous fortune. But this other takes arms against the sea of troubles, and seeks by opposing to end them. There are men whose proud and impatient spirit cannot brook the predominance of matter over mind, which the game of golf so often exemplifies. In "fractured club and cloven ball," in "foozled drives and putts not in," they see not, like their meeker brethren, the finger of Fate. These Ajaxes defy the lighting, and give tongue to the anger which consumes them.

When one has the misfortune to play against "the man with a temper," the very greatest tact and knowledge of human nature are necessary, if one is to attempt to soothe his savage breast. "Touch not the cat without the glove." But the devastating and demoralising effect of the golfing temper, on even the finest natures, is so terrible, that it is extremely dangerous to say anything, however apparently sympathetic, and the patient is much better left severely alone, until the paroxysm has passed. The breaking of the club wherewith the fatal stroke has been delivered, is a common symptom in such cases;

and usually, this sacrifice is less an act of reprisal on the club itself, than a solemn protest and testimony against the injustice of which the golfer conceives himself to be the victim, and a necessary step towards the rehabilitation of his mind. The angry golfer has been known to relieve his pent-up feelings by hurling his club far from him, after the failure of his stroke. This is an extremely dangerous habit, as, in his anger, the golfer is frequently careless of the direction in which his club flies, and his partner will do well to keep an eye on his movements. Like the "fatalist," "the man with a temper" had better be avoided, whenever possible. No pleasurable game is to be had in such company, and their habits are extremely infectious.

If players would only treat others as they would wish others to treat themselves, the harmony and pleasure of the game would be greatly enhanced. The well-balanced mind will not be unhinged by the untoward chances of golf. The wise golfer recognises, that but for these alternations of luck, the game would cease to amuse or charm, and if he has more than his share of bad luck, or bad play, to-day, he says nothing about it, being sure that to-morrow, things will go better for him. To go on inventing reasons for one's bad play is fatal to improvement, and can only annoy and irritate one's partner. "Deeds, not words," is the true golfer's motto.

"In my opinion," said a wise old caddie, "a man sud niver mak' excuses for hisself at gowf. It's like bein' disrespectfu' to Providence. Gowfers sud jist tak' things as they come and be contentit. In my opeenion some fowks like to shaw off a bit by bletherin' aboot their bad play."

> "Be not thy tongue thine own shame's orator,
> Look sweet, speak fair."

CHAPTER XIV.

CONTINENTAL GOLF.

FOR the toil-worn Briton, on holiday intent, it is always a pleasant thing, on a fine day, to sit on the upper deck of a Channel steamer, and watch the white cliffs of Albion "fade o'er the waters blue." As they sink below the horizon, all the cares and worries of the pilgrim's life, under which he has been struggling and groaning for months past, seem to slip, like Christian's load of sins, from off his back, and he arises and sniffs the salt Channel breezes, a new man. A well-lined pocket, and at least a fortnight's prospective absence, with the accompaniment of congenial society, are, of course, necessary conditions for the realisation of these beatific sensations; but if these are present, with what zest does he not look forward to the coming days! How welcome to his eyes the first glimpse

CROSSING JORDAN, PAU.

of the grey shores of France; and with what good humour and urbanity, on landing, he treats the gruff douanier; how sweet to his taste the primal *déjeuner* or dinner, on the foreign shore!

If the man be a golfer and meditate golf, he has even more reason to be pleased with himself, for he need not go empty away. It is now possible to play golf on good links at many places in France. The golf club at Pau, in the Pyrenees, was founded as long ago as 1856, and the torch lighted there has been handed on to Biarritz, Arcachon, Paramé, Cannes, Hyères, Dinard, Dieppe, and Mayville, and has even now reached Paris itself. Golf clubs now form part of every English holiday-maker's baggage on the Continent, and no longer excite the wonder and curiosity of the natives. "Le Golf," if not yet fully understood and appreciated, is at least known.

Some five years ago, the writer was on a sketching tour in South-eastern France. Amongst his other "impedimenta" was a set of golf clubs, with which he promised himself a game at Pau. The hotel porter at Arles, who brought the luggage to the Gare du Départ, and who had been acting as "caddie," in various sketching expeditions for the preceding days, pointed to the golf clubs as he received his parting tip, and said, "Pardon, m'sieu, est-ce que c'est pour la photographie?"

There is a curious and subtle charm about playing golf in France which must be experienced to be fully appreciated. One has, or had until lately, all the joy and rapture of the pioneer or missionary, while the antics and jargon of the French caddie are a never-failing source of wonder and delight.

"Non m'sieu, il ne faut pas prendre le brassy, vous irez assez loin avec le fer."

"Monsieur X. il est très fort comme joueur, il a fait le rond hier en soisante seize."

These and such-like remarks fall on the golfer's ear with a soothing and dream-like charm, difficult to explain or express. It is all so delightfully unreal, and the game, so dour and reserved in its native and wonted manifestation, sits so ludicrously on volatile Gallic shoulders. Surrounded as it is, in the Scotch mind at least, by more or less sombre associations of scenery, it seems curiously out of place, amid the sunshine and gayness of its French environment.

At Dieppe, the caddies, whose ordinary dress is the nondescript attire of the Norman gamin, surmounted by a huge "béret," have a gorgeous uniform of butcher blue, with red facings, of which they are naturally very proud. On the writer's caddie turning up, on the second morning of his visit, in his ordinary attire, he inquired of him why he had not donned his uniform; to which "Alexandre" replied with an impressive gesture, "On ne s'habille pas, le matin." Bright-eyed, charming little chaps they are, these Norman caddies, full of natural politeness, and as keen as mustard over the game. To see them racing down the braes after the balls, and to note the pleased eagerness with which they point out their whereabouts to their employers, is a pleasurable experience for one accustomed to the more careless and apathetic methods of their British brethren.

Golf at Dieppe is quite a late institution. The prosperity and trade of the town showed serious signs of waning, and civic counsels were divided, both as to the causes of its decadence, and as to what should be done to restore the place to its ancient flourishing condition. A letter from "John Strange Winter" (Mrs. Arthur Stannard), who now resides at Dieppe, advised the authorities to do three things, which, she assured them, would have the desired effect. The first, was to start a golf course; the second, was to advertise the place and its attractions broadcast; and the third, was to cease to fleece the passing stranger. To the credit of the Dieppois, this very sensible advice has been fully acted upon. A fund was soon raised, a golf course was found, and a club formed. The town is being boomed for all it is worth, and the hotel proprietors, coming to their senses, are at length bringing their tariffs down to reasonable proportions. At the Hôtel de Paris, nearest the links, the golfer will find every comfort at a pension of from 10 to 12 fr. a day, so that, even from London, a golfing holiday at Dieppe, from the point of view of expense, is but little dearer than one at Sandwich or Littlestone. The golf course is yet new, and will take a deal of work and play on it, before the golf becomes good, but the ground, if small, is of the most sporting character, the air is bracing, and the views, both to the north and south, of the rocky coast of Normandy, are exceedingly fine. In the hands of Mr. Samborne, the British pro-consul, as captain, and with Mr. Stannard as secretary, the Dieppe golf club ought to have a great future before it, as its enterprise deserves.

The golf course of Pau is the oldest, and perhaps also the best, of Continental golf courses. Though it is an inland course, so much money has been spent on it under the best direction and advice, that amongst inland courses anywhere it would take a lot of beating. It lies beautifully, by the banks of the Gave, just outside the town, and in the middle of the most enchanting scenery. Across the river to the south, vine-clad slopes and wooded hills and mountains, rising one behind the other, lead the eye away to where, in the far distance, the snow-capped and serrated edge of the Pyrenean mountains seems to pierce the heavens. The "Pic du Midi de Bigorre," which sounds Irish, but isn't—though it is a useful phrase in a bunker—dominates the distant range, and throughout the day, its rugged summit catches and holds the glittering southern sunlight. On the north, the valley is sheltered by well-wooded heights. To the east, one gets glimpses of the town, past the château and park of Henri IV., while to the west, the winding course of the Gave can be traced for miles, its banks poplar-clad, and dotted with orchard farms and stately châteaux. The climate is mild and equable in winter. Besides the golf club on the green, attached to which is the Ladies' Golf Club, there is a well-appointed and excellent English club in the town. A pack of foxhounds hunt regularly during the season, and race-meetings are also held at Tarbes. Thus either for the golfer or sportsman, Pau is an ideal wintering place.

There are hotels of all sizes and pensions galore. The Hôtel Gassion and the Hôtel de France are both of them palatial and luxurious, and there is no lack of hospitality and sociability amongst the residents. Indeed the kindness which the writer, going as a perfect stranger, received from Mr. Foster Barham, the secretary, and from other members of the English club, when he visited Pau, on a golfing holiday a year or two ago, was unstinted, and he is glad to have this opportunity of acknowledging it.

A good game of golf can always be had at Pau, for there are to be found usually, Mr. J. R. Hutchinson and Mr. R. Borcel, both excellent players, while Mr. Charles Hutchings and Mr. Horace Hutchinson are also frequent visitors. The golf course is of good length, being $3\frac{1}{2}$ miles round. The putting greens are excellent, and there are plenty of natural and artificial hazards.

From Pau to Biarritz is not a far cry, and the golfer, weary of inland golf, can easily have a round at Biarritz, and fill his lungs with the briny air of the Bay of Biscay before returning to Pau in the evening. There is much charm in Biarritz golf. The course is short and easy, although good lies through the green are rare; but the course lies high, on the top of the cliffs over the bay, and the views are magnificent. To the north, the winding coast-line of sand and cliff is merged in the forests of the Landes. The huge sweep of the bay fills the western and north-western prospects, and in a westerly or north-westerly gale the seas are superb. To the south, behind the straggling spurs of the Basses Pyrénées, the Spanish mountains are visible, and the northern coast-line of Spain stretches away westwards, till it is lost on the distant horizon.

There is a comfortable golf club situated on the course, and visitors are admitted on introduction, and on payment of a weekly or monthly fee. There is also, as at Pau, an English club in the town. The climate of Biarritz is variable in the extreme, in the winter months, but from March till September or October, it is reliable and charming, and the place is full of life and gaiety.

Quite close, but nearer the Spanish frontier, is the delightful old town of Bayonne, historically interesting from the part it played at the close of the Peninsular War, and as being the birthplace of the bayonet. The bayonet-making industry has died out, and the inhabitants now devote their energies to the making of chocolate creams of fascinating flavour, a change of "métier" which seems to be going "one better" than turning spears into pruning-hooks.

For those who wish to escape, somewhat, from the constant presence of their fellow-countrymen, and to whom golf is not everything, Bayonne is the place to stop at. Thirty minutes by tram, or ten minutes by train, take the golfer to the Biarritz golf course, and if he decide to stop at home, he will find plenty of things in Bayonne to interest and amuse him. It is the headquarters of an army corps and bristles with fortifications. There is a bull-ring, and the streets and inhabitants are picturesque in the extreme. The cathedral is beautiful, and two rivers, moving with craft of all descriptions, meet in the town, and give it, at certain points, all the appearance and charm of Venice. Within easy distance, delightful excursions may be made, across the Spanish frontier, to Fuenterrabia, Pasajes, and San Sebastian, and for residence, there is an old-fashioned French hotel, called quaintly the "Hôtel du Panier Fleuri," which, for comfort and cheapness, and the excellence of its wines and cuisine, is one of the wonders of the world.

A very good way to get to Biarritz or Bayonne, for those who do not mind the sea voyage, is to come by sea from London to Bordeaux, by the comfortable steamers of the General Steam Navigation Company, and from thence by train. The sea voyage occupies from $3\frac{1}{2}$ to 4 days.

Golf has also taken root in the Riviera, and at Cannes and Hyères there are now flourishing golf clubs. The difficulties which Englishmen experience in getting suitable ground to play golf on, in France, are enormous, and arise firstly from the absurd way in which even a small piece of land is held by a very large number of persons, all of whom require to be satisfied, and secondly from the prevalent French idea that every Englishman is rolling in money. The Cannes Golf Club, at the outset, had no fewer than thirty-six landlords, and the golfers at Dinard, before they finally succeeded in acquiring and making their present excellent course, had experiences which have been well-described by a writer in the "Golfing Annual." He says, "A Breton's one idea is to 'exploiter' the English. He considers the word 'milord' (not that they grow in great quantities at Dinard), signifies mille-or (thousands of gold)! 'Oh! dame, oui.' They must pay, '*ces Anglais.*'" In this way a piece of land may be bought or rented, everything arranged, lease signed, for a rent four times the value of the land—*cela va sans dire.* The purchaser or tenant thinks he has only to enter into possession. Poor deluded mortal! His troubles are just commencing. What on Monday belonged to one most respectable, accommodating, and generally amiable *père de famille*, has by Tuesday become the property of countless sons, daughters, brothers, and, we were going to say, wives; but at any rate cousins, to the tenth degree, uncles, aunts, and all other available relations. *Le gros* Jean, Mathurin, François, Marie, Alphonsine, Victorine, and even *la pauvre petite* Angeline must all have their share of the spoil; in short, what on one day was leased from one proprietor, has by the next become the property of a dozen, who all put forward claims to be satisfied before the Briton can make use of Breton soil. Under these circumstances, it is evident what difficulties have to be overcome by those who were deputed to arrange matters for new golf links. Even after all preliminaries were so far advanced that it was considered safe to bring over Tom Dunn to arrange the course, and the work was actually commenced, troubles were anything but over; other proprietors cropped up, enormous sums were asked for the burning of a gorse bush or a bit of dry rushes, and the unfortunate secretary, whenever he made his appearance on the course, was met by threats of a *procès*, or something equally appalling."

British pluck and patience, however, both at Cannes and Dinard, have triumphed over all difficulties. The Cannes club acquired new ground where there was but one landlord, a few minutes by rail from the town. It is 60 acres in extent, and is let on a lease of 19 years, with option of renewal. An old farmhouse in the ground has been transformed into an excellent and picturesque club-house, and the course is of a very sporting character. There is also a small putting course for ladies.

Southampton to St. Malo, is the proper route for Englishmen going to Dinard, and Dinard itself is reached by a small steamer running from St. Malo. The neighbourhood is healthy and picturesque, and the Grand Hôtel de Dinard is well appointed and moderate in its charges.

The golf course at Mayville (named after the Duchess of York) is near Boulogne, and is the nearest on the Continent to London. Though it has only lately been made, it gives promise of being one of the best of Continental golf courses. It is nearly four miles in length, and Taylor and Fernie, in consultation with whom the holes have been laid out, speak in the highest terms of its golfing qualities. Mayville will be situated—for the watering-place exists as yet mainly on paper— at the mouth of the Canche, close to the picturesque old fishing village of Etaples. It was in the estuary of the Canche that Napoleon made all his preparations for the invasion of England, and the neighbourhood is full of other interesting historic memories. Etaples, or Quentovic, as it was then called, was a favourite resort of the Romans, during their occupation of Northern Gaul and Britain. In the Middle Ages it was the scene of many a conflict between the French and the invading English, and the battlefields of Crécy and Poictiers are in the locality. With a fine golf course, a dry and bracing climate, and a situation within five hours of either London or Paris, the success and prosperity of Mayville seem assured.

There are eighteen holes at Paramé and a 9-hole course at Arcachon. At St. Jean de Luz, close to Spain, at Espinho in Portugal, in the Engadine, at Aix les Bains, Hyères, and Nice there are also young and growing clubs.

The Paris Golf Club has just been inaugurated at Maisons Lafitte, but no definite particulars can yet be given of the club and course. There is golf at Berlin, Homburg, and also at Antwerp, and at several places in Holland the Dutch are again taking to the game. This time they have copied it better, and abandoning the childish game of their ancestors, they are now "holing out" in the orthodox fashion.

CHAPTER XV.

TWENTY YEARS SINCE.

IT seems a long time ago, that year away back in the seventies, when I first handled a golf club. In the northern town where I was born, golf was an ancient institution, how ancient nobody knew, for, as in most Scotch places with a seaside links, the game had pursued an intermittent course through the centuries, and there were long periods when it had apparently died out. The local club, however, even then, had regular minutes dating back to the year of Waterloo, and there were ancient trophies and records, which gave token of much older societies that had flourished at various periods back to the fifteenth century.

In view of recent developments and the enormous popularity which the game enjoys to-day, these twenty years of golf have a curious interest, as one looks back on them. At the period of which I write, although young Tom Morris and Davie Strath were then at their best, there was comparatively little golf played, even in Scotland. Musselburgh and St. Andrews had, of course, always their quantum of players, for they were the headquarters of the "Honourable Company" and the "Royal and Ancient" respectively, and were besides the residence of all the best professional players. But in the other Scottish towns, even where there were excellent links, there were but few golfers, and the game was played with but little enthusiasm. The keenest players were of the artisan class, and the members of the local club were middle-aged and elderly business men, the lawyers, bankers, and doctors of the town, who came to the links occasionally for an afternoon round. None of these were good players, and they exhibited a most astonishing variety of style. No young man played, at least as an amateur, and as boys, we despised the game or thought nothing about it, and devoted all our schoolboy energies to cricket and football.

It was my elder brother who was the first to fall under the spell of golf. Leaving me at school, he went to college when he was eighteen, and one day, during a stroll on the links, he followed the young professional who was playing in a match. This young fellow was a fine player, with a beautiful style, and my brother, at the completion of his game, purchased a cleek from him. He now spent all his spare time on the links, and all his spare money on clubs and balls. He constantly played with the professional, and made astonishing progress. At the end of a year he joined the golf club, and signalised his entrance by winning all the club prizes from scratch in his first year of membership. These doings of his naturally excited my own curiosity and interest, and on Saturdays, when there was no cricket, I began also to go to the links, and play with a cleek which he lent me. To make a long story short, I, too, became badly bitten with the game, and many a night we sat up, remaking and hammering and painting golf balls, and practising swings before the looking-glass. Our room was at the top of the house, and its ceiling, which was rather low, soon became covered with the indentations made by our club-heads as we swung them in practice.

Our carpet, the pattern and colour of which I

can see distinctly at this moment, amongst a mass of other devices, had a number of round red spots about the size of a golf-hole, dotted at intervals of about six feet over its surface. Many a time, when Greek verbs and Latin versions became a weariness, we would put aside for a little, our Greek Lexicon or our "Liddel and Scott," and engage in a friendly golf match on our home green! The legs of the table formed hazards, and the game was to make the ball remain upon the red spot. If it passed over it, another stroke had to be played until such time as it rested fairly on "the red." The game required no little delicacy of touch, besides an intimate acquaintance with the inequalities of the floor. Then there was lofting of golf balls from the hearthrug into a hat placed on the bed, with a portmanteau behind it to stop the balls. We even tried our hands at club-making, but from lack of proper tools and appliances the results were not of a satisfactory nature. We devoured all the scanty golfing literature that was then obtainable, and all our thought and all our conversation, was of the links, of golf clubs and balls, and of young Tom Morris and the other great ones of whom we had heard.

Two things held us back and curbed our youthful enthusiasm. One was lack of cash, for golf, played even in the most economical way, costs money; and the other was a Spartan parent. My father, of whom I speak with all the tender recollection, and all the love and reverence which I feel for his memory, was one of the old school. He had never played even cricket himself—his only sport had been fishing —and he had no understanding of the fascination of the hitting of a ball. He had no sympathy with us in our sports, and always looked upon the time we devoted to them as so much taken from "our books," to the study of which he was always exhorting us. Needless to say, therefore, we played many a cricket match of which he heard no word. No matter if we had made chief score or bowled out half the other side, the subject was never mentioned in the family circle. If by any chance some report of our prowess reached his ears, his only comment was a regret that we should neglect our "books." My brother, however, though his golfing exploits, duly chronicled in the newspapers, were received in chilling silence at home, justified himself, more or less, in the parental eye, by winning a bursary at college.

This had a twofold effect, for while it mollified my father, the surplus cash, after paying college fees, provided us with the sinews of war, and we were able to pursue the game with all the ardour we felt for it.

Such was my enthusiasm for the game, that to become undisputed possessor of a cleek of my brother's, of which I only had the loan, I got up at five o'clock every winter morning, for three months, to read to him his notes and translation of the "Alcestis," while he read the text, in preparation for his examination. I reaped the benefit of this two years later, when I followed him to college, and in my second year read the same play.

In some months, I too had made great progress at the game, and our fame, travelling beyond our native city, had reached other golfing centres. One day—it was during our school vacation, and I was holidaying in the country—my brother came on a visit. He pulled a letter out of his pocket, which he gave me to read. It was as follows :—

"DEAR SIRS,—We hereby challenge you to a match at golf on —— Links any Saturday that is convenient for you. We are, yours faithfully,

"G. & H. FINLAY."

It can be imagined that this communication stirred us to our inmost depths. We knew the brothers Finlay by reputation as formidable players, almost professionals, who belonged to a mechanics' Club in — —. They were the best players in their native town, and older and more experienced men, who had played at St. Andrews and other famous links which we had never seen. Could we dare to accept their challenge? My brother was in practice, but I had not played for more than a month. We discussed the matter thoroughly, and though we were somewhat doubtful as to the result, our eagerness to see a new green decided the issue, and my brother wrote accepting the match and fixing a date.

Several other letters passed. A small sum, such as we could afford, was staked on the result, and one morning we arrived on the scene of action. The match was not to take place till two in the afternoon, and we devoted the morning to a practice round, and to making ourselves acquainted with the course. We took out the local professional, and played our ball against his. We both played shockingly, and he beat us by five up and four to play. In the course of the game he informed us that he played each of the Finlays level, and that we would have to play better than that, if we wanted to win in the afternoon. Much depressed, we went up to the hotel to get some lunch. My brother suggested some champagne, and as we found our resources would admit of it, we cracked a bottle of Moët and Chandon.

Lunch finished, we ordered a cab, as it was close upon two, and proceeded to the links. As we drove along the road, which commanded a view of the first tee, we became aware of a huge crowd gathered round it. It was a Saturday afternoon, and all the golfers in the neighbourhood and a good many of the townsfolk had assembled to see the match. There was also a rope and three policemen!

We were aghast, and almost repented our temerity in coming. However, the matter had to be gone through with, and we descended from the cab, the cynosure of every eye, and shook hands with our antagonists. Workmen-like golfers they were, of short but sturdy build, to which our stripling figures must have offered a striking contrast. Two bearded friends carried for them the implements of war. We advanced together to the first tee. The odds were six to four against us, for our friend of the morning had spread the report of our game, and was laying against us freely. My brother drove against the elder Finlay, and as we were the visitors, he drove first. All the morning he had hardly hit a good shot. His first now was a "screamer." Far and sure it flew, straight on the hole. The elder Finlay played a good stroke in reply, but not as long as my brother's. The younger Finlay played an indifferent second, and I played a very long brassy on to the green. We won the hole in four to our opponents' five.

I do not know what came to us. Whether it was the effect of the champagne, or the sudden shock of the crowd and the policemen with the rope, that nerved us to the task, I cannot say, but we simply sailed away from our challengers. We never missed anything. We drove like Trojans, our iron shots were pictures, and we holed phenomenal putts. I am ashamed to say how many holes we beat them by. The local crowd were sore dismayed, and Willie Gow, the professional, with whom I had a small bet, said to me as he paid it: "Ye —— fowks is rale deceivers!"

Having successfully upheld the honour of our native town, we returned to our studies of the autumn and winter, and our pursuit of golf, with renewed ardour. I entered the University in the autumn; and my brother and myself, making a few golfing converts among the students, and securing the patronage of the Lord Rector, who gave us a cup, started a University Golf Club. But whether it was the severe drubbing which I gave one of my professors, in a match against the local club, or whether the University authorities thought that the game had a dangerous and unsettling tendency, and was likely to interfere with due application and attendance at college, this institution did not long survive, and I am not aware that it has ever been resuscitated.

About this period, a Highland regiment was quartered in the town, and several of the officers were enthusiastic and fine players. I had by this time also joined the golf club, and many keen matches were made, in which I took part. Large sums were staked by these young bloods on the results, though, of course, a modest ball or half-crown, at the outside, was all I could afford to bet. One day a very important foursome was arranged, in which I had as my partner an Irish captain, against the professional and one of the lieutenants of the regiment. For the purposes of the match I was "skipping college," as we termed it, and about eleven o'clock in the forenoon, when I ought to have been engaged in the study of Greek, I was on the links enjoying the fresh air, and the game of golf, in the society of these agreeable gentlemen.

Now, if there was one set of men in the town that my father reprobated more than another, it was the officers of the garrison. They were idle fellows, with plenty of money, who carried themselves in the streets of the provincial town with a good deal of swagger. My father was a shy and reserved man, and their manners, coupled with the sundry reports of their extravagance and wildness, which had reached his ears, had led him to form the worst opinion of their characters. Certainly if he had known that any of us boys associated with them, he would have concluded that we were on the high road to perdition.

Conceive then, my horror, when, at the 8th hole, which was situated some distance from the town, I perceived my father about two hundred yards away, and walking in our direction. Wild thoughts of flight, or of hiding behind a whin bush, flashed through my mind, but I reflected that probably he had already seen me, and besides, I was ashamed to betray the situation to my companions. There was nothing for it but to await the course of events. My partner had to drive, and seeing my father, whom he did not know even by sight, right in the line of fire, he gave a wild Irish whoop, and shouted out "Fore!" in imperious tones. My father looked up, and, seeing the golfers, moved aside, and as we came up, we passed him at about twenty paces.

He never looked at us!

What he was doing on the links, where I had never before known him to go, I am unable to say. Whether his inveterate hatred of the military, whom he recognised, caused him to pass on without further regarding them, I cannot tell. I only know that he made no reference to the matter at the dinner-table, where I next met him, after some hours of agonising suspense. Perhaps the crime of neglecting my studies, to keep such company, was in his eyes so heinous and so paralysing that he could not contemplate it. I incline to think, however, that he never saw me at all, and I always look upon the affair as one of the most hairbreadth escapes of my life.

These were happy golfing days. A new golf club, in all its bravery of new leather and shining varnish, was our most coveted possession. With what care we tended it, and how its personality became engraved on our minds! In twenty years of golf, one must have run through some scores of wooden clubs, yet how few of those does one remember with any accuracy or distinctness. Our first possessions, on the other hand, their shape, their colour, the strokes we played with them, are abiding memories, that the lapse of time is powerless to efface.

And the gay *insouciance* with which we played! The fearless accuracy of our driving, and the inevitable simplicity of our putting, born of nerves untouched, as yet, by the struggle and hard experience of life! A friend reminded me the other day of how, in these years, I drove my tee shot, after a simple shout of "Fore!" over the heads of a whole battalion of volunteers, who were drawn up between us and the hole! That fearless confidence has, alas! departed, but enough of skill remains to satisfy a modest ambition; and the other delights of the game seem but to intensify as time goes on. The wild seaside spaces are sweeter and more restful than ever, the benty hillocks and the grassy hollows, the sights of the open landscape and the high, spreading sky, in which the lark is always singing—

> "So, still beside the tee,
> We meet in storm or calm,
> Lady, and worship thee;
> While the loud lark sings free;
> Piping his matin psalm
> Above the grey sad sea."

CHAPTER XVI.

THREE FAMOUS IRISH LINKS.

By W. J. MacGeagh.

THE progress which the game of golf has made in Ireland during the past ten years has been phenomenal. In this decade, no doubt, it has extended by leaps and bounds in England, and during the last two or three years, it has been spreading in America with all the fierceness of a prairie fire; but England and America are both rich countries and Ireland is a poor one, and as golf, relatively speaking, is an expensive game it was not to be predicted, even by the most sanguine of its adherents, that it would so soon and so extensively become the rage amongst a people, fond from the earliest times of field sports, but singularly inept and careless in respect of athletic games. In truth the Irish, though of a character versatile and exceedingly brilliant, seemed very unlikely ever to become subservient to the calm stoicism and hardheaded philosophy which golf demands from its votaries. Irish cricket is not, and never has been, and probably never will be, first class, and until about ten years ago, Irish football was a very feeble and erratic institution, though since then it has become world-famed. Practically the "masses" had no game, if we rule politics and the occasional skirmishes provided by the old open elections to be outside the pale of legitimate athletics. The "classes" hunted, and fished, and shot, no doubt, but covers were jealously guarded, rivers strictly preserved, and all the shootings were owned by the landlords, though leased occasionally to those wealthy Englishmen who had the temerity to risk their lives for a few weeks annually, in a country which they depicted to their friends, on their return home, as being eternally enveloped in the mists and fogs of the Atlantic, and towards which they set out with preparations more elaborate, and more precautionary, than would nowadays be required in the equipment of an expedition to Nova Zembla or Spitzbergen! Few of the "masses" in Ireland were able to take a serious part in its field sports; if any one did, he was looked upon askance, as a *lusus naturæ*, or ruthlessly hunted down and exterminated as a poacher. Thus sport was buried in the Irish bosom; but the gospel according to St. Andrews, has changed all this—and its acceptance has breathed life afresh into Irish athleticism. Thanks to Scottish pioneers, Ireland now has a sport in which "classes" and "masses" meet upon equal terms, and in which the peer and the peasant mutually engage, very frequently much to the disadvantage of the former.

The reason for this state of affairs, which has brought so many social advantages and amenities in its train, is not far to seek, and it may confidently and safely be attributed to the fact that nearly the entire seaboard of Ireland is peculiarly well adapted to the exercise of the game of golf, and little is needed in the way of preparation beyond the tread of the human foot.

One of the finest of these belts of natural golfing ground is to be found at Newcastle (co. Down), the terminus of the Belfast and County Down Railway, 38 miles south of Belfast. Here there is a very prosperous club, number-

NEWCASTLE, CO. DOWN.

ing some 460 members, who have lately built a handsome and substantial house for their accommodation and comfort. The links are undoubtedly the finest in Ireland. I doubt, indeed, if there are any superior in the world of golf. The hazards are in some places rather startling to weak-kneed players; but the putting greens are things of beauty.

The tee for the 1st hole—"The Corner"—is directly under those windows of the club-house which look due north. The length of the hole is 230 yards. A topped ball will perish in a bunker, 80 yards from the tee, and an otherwise imperfectly driven one will meet a similar fate 35 yards further on; but a raking tee shot leaves only a short pitch on to a very fine green, nicely guarded with a small mound, and with the regulation two putts it is a 4 hole.

The 2nd hole is 180 yards in length; but here is one of the most formidable bunkers of the entire course. One hundred yards from the tee is a huge sand hill, which rises to the height of 40 feet. The green beyond is perched up on high, hard by the sea, and a prettily pitched shot is required to reach and remain there. From this green there is a magnificent view of Newcastle. For almost six miles to the north-east there is a broad belt of fine strand, with scarcely a stone on it, while on a clear day, right to eastward, the Isle of Man is plainly visible. Looking southward, we have the Mourne range of mountains with their grand old pine-covered *doyen*, Slieve Donard, looking down with benevolent placidity upon the little straggling town of Newcastle, which for years has nestled sleepily under his *ægis*, unconscious of the development which awaited it.

The 3rd hole—"MacCormac's"—which is now played, is over 400 yards distant from the tee. There are few of the characteristic hazards on the line here; but it is necessary, after a well-hit drive and second shot, that the approach be played with accuracy, as the green, although extremely large and flat, is surrounded by a bewildering admixture of stones and sandy traps. Five is considered par play to this hole, and this figure satisfies most amateurs.

The 4th hole is 380 yards only, which to the tyro may merely seem "two of his best"; but as a series of extensive and far-reaching bunkers have to be weathered *en route*, and as the first of them prominently advertises itself, at a great height, about 150 yards from the tee, those "two best" of his will more than likely have been the two which came off in rosy dreamland the night before, rather than the "two" he will execute in daylight when showing his friend, or opponent perhaps—to draw from the familiar patter of the drawing-room conjuror—"How it's done"!

Let us, however, suppose that the tee shot has been played to all satisfaction, and that the thirty or forty steps of the ladder which make the summit of this first bunker accessible to the foot of the portly golfer have been climbed, a vista is then obtained of a country abounding in perils almost as great as those which have just been successfully negotiated. A duplicate of the tee shot—the second of the aforementioned "two best"—reaches the putting green, having just carried the guarding rampart of sand and sod, and the ball lies on a green, whose undulating beauties are the better appreciated after an approach off the brassy than off the niblick. This hole is a 4 bogey, but a very rare 4, when judged by Mr. A. H. Doleman's extremely wise theory of averages.

The 5th hole—"St. John's" (for Newcastle

possesses a saint, heaven-sent as leaven amongst its many sinners)—is 285 yards. There is a fine, hard, level space here for a good drive to take the very last inch of roll out of the ball. The green is on a high place, and is surrounded by a trappy, sandy bunker, with bent and the seashore beyond. Here the second shot needs cut, and plenty of it. The par is 4. Again a grand view of the Irish Channel presents itself to the eye of the appreciative.

The 6th hole is 450 yards. It is a long hole turning homewards, but not going there, the width of the Newcastle green being so great —nearly a mile, in fact—that a zigzag course can be, and is, here taken without any crossing, properly so called, taking place. This is a hole where a good brassy shot for the second will pay well. The green has been reached in two more than once, if club-room *post-mortem* examinations of played rounds are to be relied upon; but it is more than likely that when two such shots were hit, the force of the gale behind reached, in meteorological phraseology, about 70 miles an hour! The cloven-hoofed Colonel Bogey takes 5 to this hole and smiles in satisfaction.

The 7th is a short pitch over a bunker of pure fine sand. A wrist shot, pitched high and falling dead, enables the player to have two putts to halve with the par.

The 8th hole is worthy of more than a mere passing notice. Formerly this hole was given over to the rabbit and his extensive powers of colonisation. Dr. Magill, the present captain of the club and for many years the popular honorary secretary, discovered this ground, and, withstanding fearlessly the howls of the 20 handicap players and the dubious head-shaking of the scratch ones, tackled the matter, and swore by the nine gods to make a hole of it. First he had to subdue Bunny and eradicate the traces of his immemorial ravages. The nature of the virus with which the genial doctor inoculated Bunny may never be discovered, let Australia yearn for it as she may ; but it was effectual and Bunny was wiped out. The green-keeper has since prevailed, and the million rabbit-holes, which Mr. Horace Hutchinson alludes to in his " Famous Golf Links," have disappeared, if holes can correctly be said to disappear. However, the million holes are not there now—there is one only and a grand one it is. It is

360 yards from the tee, and there has lately been laid at great expense a fine new green. For purely scientific golf this is the best hole in the course, and after carrying over a deep dell, right in front of the tee, in which grows fern and bent, and soaring over the grassy hill upon which the direction-post is planted, a good brassy shot gets home, and 4 goes down upon the card.

The last of the outgoing nine holes, "Deception," is 276 yards, and here is a green which Hoylake, in its palmiest days, might justly envy. This green was also one of Dr. Magill's surprise packets. He laid it out darkly and by night, or at least many not over-credulous golfers so believe. Certainly he kept it dark for two years, lest perhaps he might be indicted for conspiracy with the green-keeper and his merry men. Its *locus in quo* lay entirely *off* the then existing course, though *in* the way the doctor expected the course would take, in the optimistic view he held of the possibilities of Newcastle's future. The green lay fallow for two years, and now it is an ideal one, flat as it is notwithstanding. Its youth not having been tampered with, in its maturity its verdancy is extraordinary—and it gives every promise of a hale old age.

The 10th hole is a very good one, the drive is over a chasm from which the hole takes its name. It is 245 yards, and is a 4.

The next hole takes us to the most northerly point of the course; the drive here also needs to be hit if the par of 5 is to be attained, as there is a very extensive grave right ahead for a topped shot. This hole is called the "Sheepfold," from the fact that the green formerly was enclosed as a fold. To this fact is due the abundant growth of short grass which the green possesses.

"Old Dundrum," the 12th hole, is a very long one—460 yards. There is not much difficulty en route, but the going is rather heavy, and it is a hole of very little interest. The par is 5.

The "Railway" hole, which comes next, is not a good one. Judged relatively with the other holes of this grand sporting course it is a very bad hole. Its length is 255 yards, but the approach is bad and the green is of a hog-back character, introducing a great element of luck into the approach and making the hole extremely difficult when it is placed on the summit of the hog's back and correspondingly easy when it is cut in the hollow. The par is 4.

The "Punchbowl" hole, which follows, provides grand golf. Its distance is 517 yards, and the green, when reached by the third shot, is a fine one. Rarely, however, does the third shot reach the green except it happens to be the third shot of Sandy Herd or George Pulford who each, on the occasion when they made the joint record of the green at Newcastle, had this hole in 5; 6, however, is its par.

The 15th hole is a very fine one. Its name is "The Field," and the green, which has an area of about an acre, is of extraordinary keenness and affords good wooden-putter practice.

The next hole—"Saucer"—is a long one, and skirts the railway, bearing eastwards towards the club-house. Its par is 5, and its length a quarter of a mile exactly. The green lies just to the left of the first tee.

The "Matterhorn," 170 yards, is the 17th. Ninety yards from the tee is a sand bunker 30 feet high. This, successfully carried, enables the hole to be had in 3.

The "Home" hole is 250 yards, the green is undulating, and its situation, right under the dining-room windows of the club-house, enables the finish of a match, if carried so far, to be well observed. The green is guarded by a hill which makes the approach somewhat difficult. The record of the course at Newcastle is, as previously stated, held in partnership by Alex. Herd and George Pulford at 74. These two very fine scores were made at the Irish Championship Meeting in 1896, and were the outcome of the best of the play of twenty-eight of the leading professionals. The figures are worth giving in detail, alongside the par of the green which is 79.

Herd's score reads—

   Out ... ... 3 4 4 4 4 4 3 4 5 = 35
   Home ... ... 4 4 5 3 6 4 5 3 5 = 39
              ——
              74

Pulford's reads—

   Out ... ... 4 3 5 3 5 4 3 3 3 = 33
   Home ... ... 4 5 5 4 5 5 6 3 4 = 41
              ——
              74

The par which Colonel Bogey fathers, comprises the following figures, and will be found, even by the leading amateurs, well worthy of emulation—

   Out ... ... 4 4 5 4 4 5 3 5 4 = 38
   Home ... ... 4 5 5 4 6 5 5 3 4 = 41
              ——
              79

The amateur record of the green is held by Mr.
George Combe with the following brilliant, if
somewhat erratic score—

```
Out      5 4 5 4 3 5 3 4 4 = 37
Home     2 4 6 4 8 5 5 3 3 = 40
                              ──
                              77
```

But in Mr. Combe's case it must be granted that
when he played this very fine round the 2nd,
4th, 8th, 15th, and 18th holes were played from
somewhat shortened tees.

Touching the question of accommodation at
Newcastle, while perhaps such a matter may not
quite come within the scope of a chapter on
Irish golf greens, yet (though in one's play it
is wise to take all lies with equal composure and
placidity) golfers are not all Spartans, and some
have a luxurious and epicurean side to their
nature. Have not good authorities laid it down
that above all things it is necessary that the
successful player should be well fed? So ad-
mitting this, with somewhat of shamefacedness,
it will be useful to English and Scottish players
to know that perhaps at no golfing centre in the
United Kingdom will they be so well off in this
respect as at Newcastle. In addition to the fine

club-house recently erected by the County Down Golf Club, and the already well-known hotels— the "Annesley Arms" and the "Belle Vue," which are, however, at the southern end of the village some distance from the links, the Belfast and County Down Railway Co. have just completed the building of a magnificent structure called the Slieve Donard Hotel. This imposing pile of buildings stands in its own grounds of about twelve acres, all of which are most artistically laid out. The site was selected with a fine eye to scenic effect. The chief rooms command superb views of the mountains, the bay, and the surrounding beautifully wooded country. Everything in this building is of the most modern type. The house contains about 150 bedrooms, and is lighted throughout with electricity. There is a lift for the tired golfer to every floor of the building, and there are baths of every description, from Turkish to salt-water plunge; in fact, the hydropathic department is a distinct and unique feature, and what is perhaps better than all this (good as it undoubtedly is) is the fact that the entrance hall of the hotel is not 100 yards from the railway terminus, and scarcely 100 yards from the club-house and first tee of the County Down Golf Club.

From almost the most southerly point on the County Down seaboard to the most northerly on that of the County Antrim is not a far cry in these days of comfortable and rapid transit, and here the Emerald Isle has another of its fine golf greens.

Standing upon the most elevated portion of a rocky peninsula, which is lashed unceasingly by the surges of the Atlantic Ocean, the little town of Portrush was merely the fashionable bathing resort of Ulster ten years ago, and an after-dinner promenade upon a storm-swept hill constituted its sole relaxation. In the spring of 1888 golf came as a fertilising agent, and changed the appearance of things generally and considerably. When a club was formed, and a lease of the wide stretch of natural golfing ground which runs eastward towards the Giant's Causeway obtained, Portrush began to bustle about a bit, and shook off the torpor under which it had been in the habit of lying for about eight months in every year. New houses sprang up everywhere and knit themselves into terraces and streets, the lodging-house keepers flourished exceedingly and waxed fat. The Northern Counties Railway Company went extensively into brick and mortar, and, heedless of Sam Weller's aphorism, that "buyin' houses was delicate English for goin' mad, and takin' to buildin' a medical term for being incurable," added considerably to their already extensive hotel. In 1892 the Golf Club had 400 members and £3,000 to spare, which sum was forthwith also turned into brick and stone, and ultimately fashioned into a very handsome club-house, which commands a noble view of the sea and the Giant's Causeway, and is internally replete with every comfort and convenience. There are two very fine courses at Portrush, and the ladies' course of eighteen holes is one of the very finest to be found anywhere. The long course, as extended in 1896, is a very fine one, and bad lies are an infrequent cause of bad play. In fact the nature of the ground through the green renders players who golf constantly at Portrush extremely fastidious, and liable to be considerably disappointed when, on golf intent, they wander into new pastures. Round several of the holes, notably those near the club-house and those which are skirted by the main road to Coleraine, Bushmills, and the Giant's Causeway, there has been for many years past very considerable impress by the foot of the excursionist,

of the nursery-maid and her charge, and of the
perambulating townsman, so that hereabouts the
sod is firm and true and level, and covered with
short, fine grass, though somewhat heavy withal.

The new course at Portrush is a long one, and
as it has not yet been properly advertised by
the pen of the golfing scribe or exploited by
the play club of the far-driving professional, a
task of some difficulty lies in describing it accurately. There is no better test of a course than a
two or three days' tournament for substantial
money prizes in which twenty or thirty of the
leading golfers in the world seriously engage
each other for gold or glory. This discloses the
character of a course better than reams of scrib-
bling or oceans of irresponsible conjecture,
though it is almost invariably accompanied by
a ruthless slaughter of many beautiful and inno-
cent hypotheses by very ugly yet entirely incon-
trovertible facts. Nothing so much discomposes
the local authorities as to see three or four of
their perfect "five" holes calmly annexed by
some daring young professional in four each, and
although the ruffled equanimity of the authorities is a painful sight, it is by no means an
uncommon one. Both the par which is under-

THE IRISH AMATEUR CHAMPIONSHIP, PORTRUSH, 1896.

stood and generally accepted at Portrush for its new course, and the record also, may, therefore, go on with calm and even minds until next September, when the open Amateur and Professional Irish Championship is due to be played there, but then they may be very rudely and completely shattered.

The 1st hole, treated as they all must be for our present purpose, *i.e.*, from the medal tees, is two full drives and a short iron shot to rather a good green in a triangular position between two roads. It is a 5, and is called "Glenmanus."

The 2nd hole, also a 5, is over a fine stretch of turf, and there is always a good lie for the second shot. A sliced ball may lie on a road some four feet below the level of the course, and guarded by two stone walls—a very difficult place to get back from both physically and golfically. If, however, the slice has been very pronounced, one's ball is over this road and on to the ladies' links, from whence, if counter attractions are successfully resisted, the regaining of the men's course entails no penalty beyond the distance lost. The green is a very fair one, perched up, nevertheless, in a difficult situation.

The 3rd hole has a tricky little burn to be

crossed, but it is only a good drive and an iron, and is a 4 hole. The green is a good one.

The 4th hole—"Camerons"—is a poor hole, and has no features of interest; a road has to be crossed, and the green is guarded by an artificial bunker. It is also a 4 hole.

The 5th hole—"Dunluce"—is a grand one indeed, well worthy of its historic designation. Many players hold the opinion that this hole is quite the best on the entire course, and in this the writer is entirely at one with them. The length of the hole is over a quarter of a mile, and the play space where a bad lie could not be found, is very wide. There is a small stream about 150 yards from the tee, but this should be carried, and then two more good shots will fetch the green, which is large, and it is the only one on the course which gives evidence of having been formerly tilled ground; it is nicely guarded by a little sandy bunker, which must be pitched over, and is a very good 5 hole.

The 6th hole is the first of the new holes of the course as extended in 1896. It supplants the old "Feather-Bed," and is a vast improvement upon that old and obsolete institution. It is a 5 hole, and is reached by two play club shots, nearly always obtainable, and an iron shot over a disused farm road, or "loanin"—formerly much frequented by "talking age and whispering lovers"—on to a high green.

"Primrose Dell" is the 7th hole, and requires a full straight drive to a small made green, protected on its flanks by dykes, and beyond by a stream.

The 8th hole presents two hills for carry by the tee shot. The second shot will scarcely get home, and the par may safely be considered 5.

The 9th hole may be set down as a 4, with straight driving. Time will probably provide a wider play space here, but meantime it is somewhat restricted on either side by heavy bent, fern, and broken ground. The green is in a small field, and difficult to negotiate, as a sod fence guards it, and too bold an approach will lie under a similar fence beyond.

The 10th hole, an uneventful 5, from which we proceed to "Patrick's," a capital golfing hole every way. There is a very high bunker to be carried rather close to the tee, and a second bunker, this time an artificial one, lies yawning for a topped second. The green when reached is large and true, and 4 is good to it.

Now we leave the new ground, and are back to the old course, practically speaking, except at the 16th, where the old "Chapel" hole and the "Gasworks" have been thrown into one.

"Bunker's Hill"—the 12th—will be reached on a calm day in one, and is a 3 hole.

The "Valley," which follows, is a grand hole, without, however, any distinguishing characteristic beyond that conveyed by its name. It is gratifying to the good player to hole out here in 5, and rather disappointing if he fails.

"Purgatory" requires a fine tee shot to carry the undesirable chasm which lurks for those who err, but who, happily, are not irretrievably lost. Those who lose a shot here, and with this penalty on their shoulders hole out in 5, should rejoice that worse did not befall them, as it easily might have done.

The next hole is a 4, and its annexation in that figure should fortify the player, who at the next tee has to be "thrice armed" in order to carry a fearful gully, to restrain the wanderings of his mind towards the hospitable attractions of the club-house, now in view, and to prevent his eye being attracted by the symmetrical architecture of a Roman Catholic church. All these distractions withstood, he may have a 3 hole where 4 is the par.

Now we have to cross a road to play the "Crater," the most formidable hazard on the entire course. A topped drive or a short one means grief in sand or in a brook or on a road, but a good straight tee shot gives a 3 hole, while safe pawky play to the left, and a short pitch to the green, ensures a 4.

The "Home" hole is a good drive from a high tee on to falling ground, and a brassy shot therefrom to the green, which lies just beneath the club-house windows. Portrush course affords fine scientific golf, and everything there is modern and up to date. The air at Portrush is extremely bracing, and makes early rising, after even late *séances*, absolutely no virtue at all! It is impossible to feel ill at Portrush.

The journey from Portrush to Portsalon is an interesting one, and very beautiful scenery meets the eye everywhere *en route*. First we go by rail to Coleraine, and thence, on the main line from Belfast northwards, to Londonderry. From

Londonderry there is a short half-hour's rail to Fahan, and there passage is taken on board a neat river steamer, which steams through the many lovely little bays and harbours with which Lough Swilly abounds. Portsalon is reached in an hour, so that there is ample time for lunch before starting on a round at the usual hour of two o'clock. There is first-class accommodation for over forty guests in the roomy shooting lodge which Colonel Barton, the owner of most of the land hereabouts, has turned into a hotel, and an excellently managed hotel it is too. It stands high above the harbour, and commands a beautiful view of the lough and of the links. These links are free to all guests staying in the hotel at a nominal charge of sixpence a day. Seven golfing days in the week may be had here, if the visitor is keen enough for it, for, although we are still in Ulster in Donegal, it almost requires the convincing production of an atlas to prove this to those who have travelled in the South of Ireland and are acquainted with its people. Here we are amongst pure Celts, and, though golf flourishes, the Scottish element, so abundant in Ulster generally, has been left out of sight, and while the Queen's Writ runs in

Donegal the *anathema maranatha* of the General Assembly does not, and erring Scotsmen, having escaped from its jurisdiction, have more than once engaged on a Sunday with the profane native in a good tussle over eighteen holes. Scruples are gently broken down, first by putting on the home green, then by short approaches to the next, until finally, for his holiday here, at all events, the genial Sabbatarian strays far from the principles of his forbears.

The 1st hole—"The Lodge"—is 150 yards in length—a good cleek shot. The green is small, and one must not pull the shot, or down a hill and in the emerald waters of Lough Swilly will be its resting-place. To be too far also has its dangers and difficulties in bent, but anywhere to the right is safety, and although a 3 should be obtained, more frequently a 4 will be the figure appearing on the scoring card, though 3 is the par.

The driver is required to the 2nd, which rejoices in the mellifluous name of "Meliamore," and is 319 yards in length. There is space all round here for the drive, and right or left there are no difficulties if the tee shot has been well hit. Two "considerable swipes," as Transatlantic golfers say, will reach this green, which is almost on a level with the strand, and hard by the sea. It is fast and true, and this is a 4 hole.

The 3rd hole—" Strand "—is 275 yards long, and is beset by difficulty, on the right by a winding river, and on the left by the strand and the falling ground leading to it, so that careful rather than brilliant play is required here, and this makes the hole a 4, though an easier 4 than the preceding hole.

"Greenfort"—so called from its proximity to Colonel Barton's residence—is 323 yards in length. The green is perched up on high, and the ground rises all the way from the tee, in front of which a rather wide river runs. The locals call this a 5 hole, but it is often taken by perfect golf in 4.

The 5th hole is aptly called " Desert." One drives off from a high place into space and over rocks, boulders, stones, sand, and bent. The distance is set down as 195 yards, but a lesser number would probably be nearer accuracy. The green is a good one, and as it is cuppy a long straight drive will remain there, and reward the player with his second 3.

Now for a hole called " Stocker," an abbreviation, no doubt, of Ballymastocker, the name of the little horseshoe bay where the dancing sunlight encourages the player who is up and consoles the one who is down. It is the prelude to a rather long and narrow valley, where the play space is greatly restricted on either side by bent, heavy grass, and numerous little demon rocks scattered through the ground as if they had been sown there and had taken sound root and were going to yield a healthy and fruitful crop. Careful play, however, rewards one with a 4. The green is good, and is guarded by a grassy mound.

Hole No. 7, designated "Valley No. 1," is a good hole every way, though its 330 yards are uneventful. It should be reached in 2, and is a 4 hole with first-class play.

"Valley No. 2"—the 8th—is a short hole, set down at a generous 160 yards, though frequently reached with the iron, and a light one at that! It is no more than a 3, so after holing it in that number, we have eight holes in 29, and have to play the 9th—a long hole, 504 yards, called "Dunree." This is the best hole in the course, and the credit for this fine sporting hole is unquestionably to be assigned to Dr. O'Brien, one of the best of Irish golfers and good fellows. This hole was formerly much shorter, and had a wretched green perched up in an impracticable place. A new green has been made 100 yards farther afield, and by adding length to this hole 80 to 90 yards are added to the 10th. The drive for this 9th is off a high place, and there is everywhere a good lie for the second shot, which should be played short with the cleek to avoid pitching into the river, which has to be crossed once more here. With care and accuracy and good driving this hole can be made in 5, but 6 is good golf to it, and 6 added to 29 makes 35—a fine score for the first nine holes of this picturesque course.

Now we are homeward bound, and now the gods must be propitiated or they will turn their faces from us, and grief will be our portion, for we are now in a region of "alkali sage and desert" and pumice-stone like little rocks and sandy trappy places where the putting greens come upon us unawares and suddenly as one might stumble upon derelict holy carpets on the outskirts of the Great Sahara; we may come home here in 36, covered with glory, or we may leave the bones of our wooden clubs whitening amid its steppes, and the fragments of our scoring cards the sport of every wind that sweeps it!

The 10th, which we now play, is called "Drumany," and is set down as 260 yards long. It is an easy 4 hole, there being no difficulty *en route* except perhaps rather heavy ground to the left, and a trappy scooped-out bunker to the right.

"Killevee," the 11th hole, is not a good one by any means. The tee shot, if good, will not be interfered with, but when the brassy is taken in hand a considerable difficulty confronts the player. Unless the drive has been off the line to the right, it is impossible to reach the green without having to cross a rather deep though scattered belt of rocks. Here, after a fine second shot, the ball may be in a perfectly unplayable place not many yards from the pin on the hither side of the green, or if too bold be the approach it meets with equal disaster. The length of the hole is 300 yards, and it should be a 4 to a first-class player; but on account of the rocky dangers amongst which the green lies, as it might be by a freak of nature, the player who takes his iron, plays his second shot short, and then pitches a pawky mashie shot on to the green, will in nine cases out of ten have the better of the first-class player who tries to reach the green with his second, and who suffers by its restricted area and surrounding dangers. This hole is a good 4.

The 12th hole is called the "Altar," and is a cleek shot on to a hill, where there is a very good green. It is a 3 hole, sometimes a 2.

The 13th—"Craigmore"—is a very difficult hole; the drive must be perfectly straight, or it will be foundered in heavy ground to the right, or be down a steep gully to the left. The green is very small, and is surrounded by the characteristic small, volcanic-like, rocky boulders. The player is lucky who has a 4.

Now for the 14th—the "Bin"—we get another iron shot on to a hill, the hither side of which is pure, fine sand. This is one of the best greens on the course, and altogether a nice short hole. On the far side of the green there rises to the height of 40 feet a fine rocky cliff, smothered in moss and fern, and growing ash, blackthorn, primroses, and wild hyacinth in a profusion of prismatic colours so gorgeous as to make the golfer with artistic instincts pause and catch his breath with wonder and delight. For is it not better to attribute his pause to his artistic instincts than to a very commonplace desire to regain his wind after climbing knee-deep through the sandy tract which lies between the tee and the green? This hole counts 3.

The 15th hole—"Matterhorn"—is 240 yards, and is an easy 4.

The "Alders" is next, and measures 380 yards; the green is on falling ground, and the direction crosses the fourth hole at right angles. It is a fine hole, however, and the green is guarded by the river. It is a 5 hole.

The 17th, which we have now reached, is a good hole, long and sporting; the "River" is its designation, and the river has to be crossed from the tee and continually avoided on the left during the 430 yards we have to traverse before reaching the green. This river is one of the features of the course, and the golfer who completes 17 holes without his ball having sought its depths is lucky. It is a good 5 hole.

The "Home" hole measures 260 yards, and brings us to the hotel entrance gate. It is a 4, and our score home reads 36, and our total for the round 71. This no doubt is an excellent score, a very rare one on any course, but yet by no means an impossible one for Portsalon, and one which Herd or Sayers, or Mr. Hilton might readily make on an occasion, and yet be 80 or 85 next time of trying. George Pulford, of Hoylake, holds the record of the course at 76, and he is the only one of the professionals in the first flight who has ever played there.

Naturally there are several other capital greens in Ireland, both seaside and inland; the best of the latter being the *habitat* of the Malone Golf Club, Belfast, and of the former, those at Buncrana, Dublin, and Lahinch; also a fine course at Carnalea, the home of the Royal Belfast Golf Club—9 holes only, but the mother club of golf in Ireland must not be overlooked! None of these courses, however, either in point of perfect suitability for the game or of grandeur of scenery—except, perhaps the charming links of the North-West Club at Buncrana—can compare with the three famous greens which loyal Ulster grapples to her soul with hooks of steel, at the same time always holding forth to players from whatever country they hail, who come to visit them, the open hand of fellowship, and greeting them with a *cead mille failthe*.

CHAPTER XVII.

GOLF IN AMERICA.

GOLF in the United States is the amusement of the well-to-do classes alone, and there is nothing on this side of the Atlantic to compare with the public commons on which golf is played in the British Isles. It is true that there are free links at Franklin Park, in Boston, and at Van Courtland Park, in New York City, but the golf that they furnish is of an indifferent order, and the general public has consequently been slow to realise the possibilities of the game. One must belong to an expensive club if he wishes to play golf, and of course this entails initiation fees, annual subscriptions, and the various other expenses incidental to club membership. The poor man has no place as yet among American golfers, and the sport remains as distinctly exclusive as is polo or yachting. The big clubs have immense sums invested in land and buildings. Their running expenses are very heavy, and the charges for coaching, supplies, club-making, and the like are ridiculously out of proportion to their actual value. Willie Dunn is reported to have said that the expense of making the first putting green of the Ardsley course (Dobbs Ferry-on-Hudson) was equal to the entire cost of the average 9-hole course in Great Britain. The Morris County, Knollwood, Shinnecock Hills, Chicago, and St. Andrews Clubs, are among those owning their own land, and the average sum invested is not far from $100,000, equivalent to a very respectable ground-rent. The Newport, Ardsley, Ouwentsia (Chicago), Philadelphia County, Essex County, Shinnecock Hills, and Chicago Clubs all possess magnificent club-houses, fitted up with sleeping apartments, grill-rooms, and every possible luxury and convenience. Naturally all of this costs money, both to establish and to maintain, and it makes golf an expensive amusement, far too expensive for the man of moderate means. A season subscription at the Shinnecock Hills Club costs $60 for a man and his wife, and for each additional member of his family he must pay an extra $15. If he puts a friend up at the club the charge is $1 a day for the mere privilege of playing over the course.

Since golf has been made a fashionable fad, it is perhaps inevitable that its development in America should have been along these lines of outward show, but it must not be inferred that the element of genuine sport has been entirely overlooked. Golf is played for its own sake; if it were not so, not a club-house in the United States would open its doors for another season. Golf has been accepted upon its merits, and it is only a question of time when it will take its place upon the calendar of national sports, and be within the reach of every one who cares to handle a club. Moreover, the tennis and field clubs are all taking up the game in obedience to the growing demand, and are laying out short courses as a side issue to baseball and tennis. And in many cases golf is rapidly supplanting its older rivals, and play-clubs and mashies are more in evidence than are bats or rackets. Most of these smaller clubs belong to the United States Golf Association, and their membership is largely composed of the younger people. Their initiation dues and subscriptions are on a comparatively moderate scale, averaging $10 yearly, and it is upon their courses that the boys and girls of the rising generation are learning to appreciate and to play the game.

Golf in America had its first real beginning in 1887, when Mr. John Reid and Mr. Robert Lockhart, two expatriated Scotchmen, started in to play the game on some pasture land near the city of Yonkers, N.Y. Ten years before that, Mr. Charles B. Macdonald had tried to introduce the game in Chicago, but he made no converts, and finally gave it up in despair. Mr. Reid and his "Apple-tree" gang, as it was styled in affectionate raillery, had better success, and in 1888 they organised themselves into the St. Andrews Golf Club, and laid out a regular 9-hole course. The club grew steadily in numbers and enthusiasm, and in 1894 they took the lease of an old farm, remodelled the dwelling-house for club use and laid out a new and better course, although still one of 9 holes. And now, in the autumn of 1897, the club has just taken possession of what they hope will be a permanent home. The new course of 18 holes is at Mount Hope, on the Putnam railway, twenty miles from New York City, and the club property embraces a tract of

ST. ANDREWS CLUB-HOUSE, MOUNT HOPE, NEW YORK.

160 acres of the picturesque Westchester County. The course is over 5,000 yards in playing distance, and possesses grand possibilities for good golf. The turf is excellent, being old pasture land, and the hazards are nearly all natural ones. The putting greens are 100 feet square, and will be very good and true in time. There is hardly a hole that can be said to come under the category of "levellers," and good long driving is consequently the prime essential for a low score. It has been the aim of the club to create a course that shall conform as nearly as possible to Old World standards, with the idea that their St. Andrews may assume the same premiership in the American golfing world that *the* St. Andrews holds abroad. An impartial observer must, however, put in a demurrer in favour of the Chicago Club's course at Wheaton, Ill. The latter certainly gives better all-round golf, but then it has had the start of St. Andrews by several years, and no golf course can be made in a summer. St. Andrews may yet take the lead as the course is developed under the searching analysis of actual play. The present playing length of the separate holes is as follows :—1st, 306 ; 2nd, 293 ; 3rd, 274 ; 4th, 344 ; 5th, 308 ;

6th, 328 ; 7th, 411 ; 8th, 137 ; 9th, 370 ; 10th, 199 ; 11th, 365 ; 12th, 272 ; 13th, 190 ; 14th, 220 ; 15th, 160 ; 16th, 235 ; 17th, 415 ; 18th, 205 ; total, 5,032 yards.

The well-known players of the St. Andrews Club include : W. H. Sands, L. B. Stoddart (amateur champion in 1894), James Park, J. R. Chadwick, A. M. Robbins, John Reid, jun., H. L. Sweny and F. W. Menzies. The initiation fee is $100, and the annual subscription $30. The membership limit is fixed at 400.

Golf on Long Island was introduced in the spring of 1891 by Mr. Duncan Cryder and Mr. Edward Mead, two members of the Southampton Summer Colony, who had seen and played the game at Biarritz. A course of twelve holes was laid out over the rolling hills and sand-dunes of the Shinnecock Hills, and so enthusiastically was the game taken up that a club-house was built at once, and in September of the same year the club became the first regularly incorporated golf club in the United States. Since then the club-house has been twice enlarged, over 100 acres of land have been acquired by purchase, and the course has been lengthened to the regulation eighteen holes. There is also a short course of nine holes for the ladies, and no woman may play over the long course until she has qualified by making the "red" course three separate times in a certain minimum number of strokes.

In its general features Shinnecock approaches more closely to Scottish ideals than any other American course. Nearly all our leading clubs are inland ones, but Shinnecock is on the Long Island coast, between Peconic and Shinnecock bays, and the course runs over real seashore links. It is true that the turf of the fair green cannot be compared to that of the old country, but it is improving with care and cultivation. There are no unfair traps in the way of trees and stones, and the wind is an omnipresent hazard. The embankment of the Long Island railway (which is crossed four times), and artificial cop bunkers, are the principal difficulties of the course, and the total length is 5,369 yards. The greens, however, are small, and several of them have been artificially levelled up and terraced. Shinnecock was the scene of the amateur championship meeting of 1896, when Mr. H. J. Whigham, an old Prestwick player, carried off the first honours. It is good sound golf that is played at Shinnecock, and the course has been greatly improved by its extension. The holes now run:—1st, 291; 2nd, 277; 3rd, 248; 4th, 228; 5th, 162; 6th, 308; 7th, 357; 8th, 354; 9th, 489; 10th, 413; 11th, 231; 12th, 203; 13th, 368; 14th, 384; 15th, 370; 16th, 260; 17th, 214; 18th, 212; total, 5,369 yards.

The club is a stock company, and no one can be elected a member unless he or she be the owner of at least one share ($100 par value) of the capital stock. The stock may be transferred at will, but the vendor thereby ceases to be a member of the club, and the purchaser must undergo the usual process of election by ballot. The limit of the regular membership is fixed at 75, and there are now 71 names upon the roll. The initiation fee is $200, and the dues $40. There are a large number of season subscribers, who pay $60 for a man and his wife, and $15 for every additional member of the subscriber's family. The club numbers among its playing members: Mrs. Charles Brown, winner of the first woman's championship (1895); Miss Beatrix Hoyt (champion for 1896 and 1897), and Mrs. Arthur B. Turnure, runner-up in 1896. The best-known players among the men are: Dr. H. Holbrook Curtis, R. H. Robertson,

H. G. Trevor, and W. R. Betts, runner-up at Chicago in 1897.

In 1893 a score of ladies associated themselves into what is now known as the Morris County Golf Club. They put up a pretty colonial club-house, laid out a seven-hole course, and invited their men friends to give the new game a trial. To make sure of success they also provided tennis courts and a croquet ground. The men came, condescended to take a turn around the course, and surrendered at discretion. The tennis nets have not been taken out of the closets for three years, and the croquet court is now the home putting green.

In 1896 the constitution of the club was changed, papers of incorporation were taken out, and the men assumed the direction of affairs. Some ninety odd acres of land were acquired by purchase, and the course was lengthened to a playing distance of over 6,000 yards. It now ranks with the best of the inland courses, and was chosen as the arena of the woman's championship meeting in 1896.

Being an inland course, stones and trees are largely in evidence, but the turf of the mid-green is excellent, and the trenches of the artificial bunkers are filled with real sand. Water hazards are wanting, but the well-known "Punch-bowl" and the line of the Lackawann railway help to make the round an interesting one. The full course is not as yet in use, but the temporary playing distance is as follows :—1st, 230 ; 2nd, 175 ; 3rd, 232 ; 4th, 357 ; 5th, 305 ; 6th, 350 ; 7th, 235 ; 8th, 300 ; 9th, 160 ; 10th, 450 ; 11th, 450 ; 12th, 310 ; 13th, 333 ; 14th, 159 ; 15th, 157 ; 16th, 193 ; 17th, 193 ; 18th, 270.

The membership of the club is divided into two classes, regular and associate, and there are 123 names on the first list and 293 on the second, or 416 in all. Regular members must be stockholders in the organisation, which is capitalised at $50,000, the par value of the shares being $100. Both the regular and associate members pay annual dues of $25, and the initiation fee is fixed at $50. Candidates for membership must be, in the case of men, at least 18, and in the case of women at least 16 years of age. Election is according to ordinary club methods, the board of directors voting by ballot, and two black balls excluding. There is also a small list of honorary members.

The Knollwood Golf Club at Elmsford, in

MORRIS COUNTY CLUB-HOUSE, NEW JERSEY.

Westchester County, N.Y., is situated in a favourite residential section, and is within three-quarters of an hour railway journey from New York City. The club owns about 100 acres of ground, and the club-house is a handsome building and admirably appointed, having both restaurant and sleeping accommodation. The course is one of eighteen holes, laid out over rolling country, and measuring 4,466 yards in playing distance. Swamps, brooks, and roads make up the principal hazards, and the artificial cop bunkers are distinguished for their enormous proportions. They look like military earthworks, and are responsible for many a torn-up score card. The greens are of the largest size and very true and good, but there are far too many of the terraced and artificially levelled-up variety. The fair green is rather rough, but is improving under the steam-roller, which the Green Committee keep pretty steadily at work. Golfing at Knollwood is interesting work, but the punishment is often unduly proportioned to the crime, and the level greens give but little opportunity for the exercise of science in putting. The playing distance of the separate holes:—1st, 247; 2nd, 247; 3rd, 345; 4th, 400; 5th, 425; 6th,

246; 7th, 196; 8th, 150; 9th, 317; 10th, 154; 11th, 169; 12th, 154; 13th, 257; 14th, 196; 15th, 238; 16th, 356; 17th, 197; 18th, 172; total, 4,466 yards.

The membership is limited to 75, and there are about 70 names now upon the list. The initiation fee is $50, and the same amount is charged as the annual subscription.

The Chicago Golf Club has at Wheaton (a suburb of Chicago) what is undoubtedly the finest golf course in all America. It has been laid out in strict conformity to accepted old-world conditions, and the result is highly creditable to the care and good judgment of Mr. C. B. Macdonald and his associates. Of course the quality of the soil is different from that of St. Andrews and Prestwick, but the turf is excellent; a good drive is hardly ever punished by a bad lie; the hazards are of the proper sort, consisting chiefly of sand bunkers, with an occasional water-jump; there are no trees, stones, or buildings upon the course, and, above all, the holes are laid out in such a way as to virtually eliminate the element of chance. The playing length foots up 5,877 yards, the longest hole being 560 yards, and the shortest 129 yards.

A certain well-known and popular member of the club holds what is certainly one kind of a record for this same short hole. During a recent medal competition he drove eleven balls into the pond before he succeeded in getting one over, and his score for the hole was 25.

The general plan of the course is that of a double round, along the sides of a quadrangle, with the club-house and polo field on the fourth side. The amateur championship for 1897 was decided upon the Chicago Club's course, Mr. H. J. Whigham, of the neighbouring Onwentsia Club, winning even more easily than at Shinnecock the year before. The playing length in detail is as follows:—1st, 337; 2nd, 327; 3rd, 319; 4th, 390; 5th, 328; 6th, 560; 7th, 300; 8th, 268; 9th, 138; 10th, 129; 11th, 242; 12th, 308; 13th, 513; 14th, 334; 15th, 350; 16th, 317; 17th, 347; 18th, 314. The "Bogey" is 41 for both out and in.

The list of leading players includes: Charles B. Macdonald, V. Shaw Kennedy, G. S. Willits, B. M. Wilson and H. Alward.

Members must be shareholders in the organisation, the limit of membership and the number of shares being fixed at 250, the par value of the shares being $200. The yearly dues are $40 for regular members. Temporary subscribers pay $50 annually, and the clergy and officers of the army and navy $25. There are about 200 members and a small list of subscribers.

A few miles away, at Lake Forest, are the grounds of the Onwentsia Golf Club, also an 18-hole course, and inferior in playing value only to that of the Chicago Club. The plan of the course bears a striking relation to the lines of a spider's web, with the polo field as its centre, and the playing distance is 2,727 yards out and 3,006 yards in, or 5,733 yards in all. The "Skokie river" and plantations of trees are the principal natural hazards, and the few artificial ones are placed with excellent judgment. The 8th hole (275 yards) is remarkable in that the line of play makes a right angle before the green is within the range of practical politics. The distances :—1st, 388; 2nd, 183; 3rd, 485; 4th, 215; 5th, 195; 6th, 300; 7th, 338; 8th, 275; 9th, 350; 10th, 445; 11th, 400; 12th, 510; 13th, 345; 14th, 323; 15th, 327; 16th, 140; 17th, 300; 18th, 210.

Prominent among the Onwentsia playing members are : H. J. Whigham (amateur champion for 1896 and 1897), D. R. Forgan, W. B. Smith, and Lawrence Tweedie.

The club is managed as a stock company, but there are several classes of members who may enjoy the privilege of the house and grounds, although they have no voice in the management of the club affairs. The initiation fee is $100, and men pay yearly subscriptions of $35; non-residents pay $50 initiation and $20 in dues. Unmarried women and widows pay $100 initiation and $10 as an annual subscription. Boys (from twelve to twenty-one years of age), pay annual dues of $10, but they must be sons or brothers of active members. The wives, daughters, and sisters of members are admitted upon payment of $10 annual dues. The limit of active membership is fixed at 300, and there are now 254 regular, 1 life, 1 non-resident, 7 army and navy, 2 honorary, and 6 women members, or 274 in all, and exclusive of the junior enrolment.

Next upon the list of eighteen-hole courses comes Ardsley, the Millionaires' Club, as it is sometimes called. The club grounds are at Dobbs Ferry-on-the-Hudson, and the club owns a magnificent piece of property stretching for half a mile along the banks of the beautiful river and then running back into the country. All the land in this section is held at enormous figures, and the Ardsley course, in its first cost and subsequent improvement, is probably the most valuable piece of golfing property in the world. Willie Dunn was employed to lay out the course (at first one of nine holes), and he was given *carte blanche* in the matter of expense. A perfect army of workmen were busy for months in felling trees, filling up ravines, and otherwise preparing the ground for the game, and the result of their labours is both beautiful to the eye and good golf as well. In 1897 nine more holes were added, the total length of the course being now 6,020 yards. There are, perhaps, too many trees on the course to suit the wild driver, but the man who will keep the line is pretty sure to be rewarded by an excellent lie. The "Alps" are a curious group of artificial grassy bunkers invented by Dunn. They have the appearance of miniature mountains, and certainly no Scottish golfer ever saw anything like them. But they add variety to the scene, and Dunn had to find some way of giving his patrons their money's worth. The first putting green is another remarkable bit of work. A good portion of a deep ravine had to be filled up, and then backed with heavy logging to prevent landslips. From below it looks very much like a stockade of the old Puritan days. The cost of the work alone on these first nine holes was not far from $50,000. The new holes are not so distinguished for their freaky features, but are quite as good golf. The distances follow:—1st, 205; 2nd, 225; 3rd, 290; 4th, 122; 5th, 375; 6th, 275; 7th, 183; 8th, 410; 9th, 260; 10th, 370; 11th, 350; 12th, 150; 13th, 270; 14th, 250; 15th, 400; 16th, 460; 17th, 350; 18th, 500.

The club-house is one of the largest and best-appointed club buildings in the United States, and contains sleeping-rooms, a large swimming tank, concert hall, grill rooms, and every other possible convenience. The club has its own railway station, and also a private dock on the river front.

Members must be the owners of at least ten shares of the capital stock, or in lieu of that pay an initiation fee of $1,000. Associate members pay $100 initiation and $75 annual dues. Subscribers pay $60 in yearly subscriptions. There are about 200 regular members and 150 subscribers.

The original course of the Philadelphia County Club at Bala, Penn., was one of nine holes, and the following newspaper description of its peculiarities will sound oddly in the ears of the golfer whose idea of what a links should be are founded upon the classic conditions of St. Andrews and Westward Ho!—

"A player who has done a round at the County Club will have passed over various points of avenue, steeple-chase course, race track, polo field, and pigeon-shooting grounds; he will have come triumphantly through a purgatorial stone-wall jump and bastion, a water-jump, and finally a vast gravel-pit or crater. . . . Stone walls, ploughed fields, quarries, fences, and chasms are among the other excellent sporting requirements of the course." Magnificent indeed, but hardly golf, seeing that a golfer is neither a jockey nor a quarryman.

But we have changed all that, and the club has now a really fine course of eighteen holes, measuring some 5,600 yards in playing distance. The club owns nearly 100 acres of land, and the club-house possesses every possible comfort and convenience. Racing, polo, and pigeon shooting still figures as fixtures upon the calendar, but golf, as is eminently proper, continues to lead them all in point of popularity.

The well-known players include Louis Biddle, J. Wilmer Biddle, G. T. Newhall, Charles and Francis Bohlen, and Mahlon Hutchinson.

The club has over 600 names upon its membership list, divided into three classes of resident, non-resident, and army and navy. Resident members pay $50 in annual dues, and the other classes $25.

The club at Newport, Rhode Island, was organised in 1893, and its magnificent clubhouse was erected in 1895. The latter is probably the handsomest and most luxuriously appointed club-house in all the world of golf, and it is the social centre of Newport's well-known Summer Colony. The polo field and the tennis courts of the Casino are almost deserted, and the World and his wife think only of their daily pilgrimage to the links.

The latter, although almost overshadowed by the magnificence of the club-house, are yet very good golf, and were the scene of the first national amateur meeting in 1895. The original course was one of nine holes, but it has since been extended to eighteen. The "Reef," the "Quarry," and the "Orchard," are the most interesting of the holes, but all are good, and the new part of the course is rapidly coming into condition. Following is the playing distance for the separate holes :—1st, 185 ; 2nd, 375 ; 3rd, 360 ; 4th, 110 ; 5th, 420 ; 6th, 350 ; 7th, 400 ; 8th, 375 ; 9th, 150 ; 10th, 215 ; 11th, 365 ; 12th, 172 ; 13th, 188 ; 14th, 340 ; 15th, 485 ; 16th, 300 ; 17th, 330 ; 18th, 325 ; total, 5,445 yards.

The club is a stock company, but the house is owned by a separate corporation, the Newport County Club. The golf club is therefore the lessee of the County Club. The membership of the club is limited to 250, and the list now stands at 122. The entrance fee is $100, and the annual subscription is $40. In addition to the active members, there are associate members who subscribe for the season, month, week, and day. The leading players include : R. Terry, jun., W. Rutherfurd, Victor Sorchan, L. Waterbury, and Foxhall Keene.

The best of the nine-hole courses is undoubtedly that of the Meadowbrook Hunt Club, of Long Island. The links are laid out over the breezy and treeless Hempstead plains. The soil and putting greens are of excellent golfing quality, but perhaps the chief merit of the course is the good judgment shown in the playing distances of the separate holes. There are no stones or break-clubs on the course, and one may use his play-club without fear that some unseen obstacle may work it irretrievable damage. The playing distance is 2,756 yards, divided as follows :—1st, 308 ; 2nd, 110 ; 3rd, 387 ; 4th, 160 ; 5th, 266 ; 6th, 296 ; 7th, 414 ; 8th, 529 ; 9th, 288. The improvements now being made upon the course will bring the playing length up to 2,873 yards.

There is only a small locker building and workshop on the links, but the handsome house of the Hunt Club is not far away, and within its hospitable walls the weary golfer may find every creature comfort. O. W. Bird, Richard Peters, T. O. Beach, and J. A. Stillman, are the leading players in the club.

The nine-hole course of the Essex County Club at Manchester, Mass., was the scene of the third annual woman's championship (1897). The length of the course is 2,565 yards, divided as follows :—1st, 370 ; 2nd, 250 ; 3rd, 400 ; 4th, 210 ; 5th, 260 ; 6th, 240 ; 7th, 286 ; 8th, 264 ; 9th, 285. Of the course in general it may be said that it is difficult, not so much from its actual

T

length as the fact that every hole is guarded by an obstacle of some sort that prevents a half-taken shot being as good as a properly lofted one. Most of the artificial bunkers are filled with clean, white sand, from which a ball may be played with one good stroke. The putting greens are good and true, and big enough to allow for a long pitch from a mashie up to the hole. The course is now being extended to eighteen holes.

George McSargent is champion of the club, and other scratch players are: Quincy A. Shaw, R. F. Tucker, C. A. Pierce, Francis J. Amory, and Nicholas Longworth. Miss N. C. Sargent is the lady champion of the club, and was the silver medallist in the woman's championship meeting for 1897. Members must be stockholders in the organisation, and the yearly subscription is $100. There are about 250 members on the list.

The foregoing rank as the leading clubs of the country, although there are perhaps a dozen others that might deserve notice. Baltusrol is a good eighteen-hole course, and Lakewood, Washington, Myopia, Philadelphia Cricket, Westchester County, Fairfield County, Lenox, Oakland, Richmond

County, Rockaway Hunt, Seabright, and Essex County (New Jersey), may be ranked among the leading clubs that have nine-hole courses. There are 89 clubs in the U.S. Golf Association, 17 associate, and 72 allied members. But this numerical statement gives no idea of the real spread of the game, since only about one-tenth of the total number of links throughout the country are listed by the Association. The latter's influence, however, is paramount in all matters of legislation and interpretation, and it is universally regarded as the governing body.

The Association was organised December 22, 1894, five clubs—St. Andrews, Brookline, Shinnecock Hills, Newport, and Chicago—being the original and charter members. The associated clubs pay annual dues of $100, and have two votes each at the annual and special meetings. The allied clubs pay $25 yearly, and may send a delegate to the meetings, but their representatives have no vote. The general direction of affairs is vested in an executive committee, made up of the officers of the Association. The late Theodore Stavemeyer was the first president of the Association, and was succeeded by Lawrence Curtis, of Brookline. R. Bage Kerr, of Lakewood, is the secretary, and Samuel L. Parrish, of Shinnecock Hills, is the treasurer of the Association.

The combination of match and medal play introduced last year at the amateur championship meeting, has been entirely successful in practice, and has been adopted at all the minor tournaments held by the individual clubs. The entire field play a preliminary medal round of thirty-six holes, and the sixteen players making the best scores are paired in match games of eighteen holes until but two contestants remain. The final match is one of thirty-six holes. The championship trophy is awarded to the custody of the winner's club, and medals of gold, silver, bronze (2), are given to the four leaders. The amateur champions: 1894, Mr. L. B. Stoddart; 1895, Mr. Chas. B. Macdonald; 1896, Mr. H. J. Whigham; 1897, Mr. H. J. Whigham.

The open championship is conducted under medal rules, and consists of thirty-six holes. The winner receives a gold medal, $150 in money (or in plate if won by an amateur), and the custody of the championship cup. The second, third, fourth, and fifth men receive $100, $50, $25, and $10 respectively. The open champions: 1894,

Willie Dunn; 1895, Horace Rawlins; 1896, James Foulis; 1897, Joseph Lloyd.

The colleges have also taken up the game, and the Inter-collegiate Association, composed of Harvard, Princeton, Yale, Columbia, and the University of Pennsylvania held its first championship meeting on the Ardsley course last July, L. P. Bayard, of Princeton, winning the individual championship, and Yale the team honours.

CHAPTER XVIII.

LADIES' GOLF.

By Miss A. B. Pascoe.

THE origin of ladies' golf may be carried back to a period coeval with man's, if we sanction the hypothesis that fathers, husbands, and brothers of those early days resembled the male relatives of our own, and gave old balls, discarded clubs, and unprofessional advice to any maiden who showed a tendency to chase feather and leather into holes, rather than to practise on the virginals, or embellish tapestry frames. Furtively, then, there has ever been a woman golfer; unrecognised, unhandicapped, unadorned with medals, she drove her ball through the air behind my lord and holed out in two, while he paid for a bumper of his favourite claret. Happy, prehistoric female, who lived her golfing life, un-

MISS AMY PASCOE.
(*Lady Champion, 1896.*)

conscious of short links, the struggles for silver-backed hair-brushes, Brigg's "brolleys," photograph frames, and all the *Sturm und Drang* of an open meeting!

When we leave the hypothetic, though probable, and enter the historic period, we find our game has a royal patroness. Mary, Queen of Scots, whose Stuart ancestors were golfers, played in the fields round Seton Palace in 1567. That even earlier in the same century golf had elicited the approval of another queen, is proved by a very interesting letter of Katherine to Cardinal Wolsey, written at the time King Henry VIII. invaded France. I am indebted to the Rev. Mr. Kerr's valuable book on "Golf in East Lothian" for this epistle, dated August 13, 1513; it is as follows: " Master Almoner, from hence I have nothing to write to you but that you be not so busy in this war as we be here incumbered with it. I mean that touching my own concerns, for going further, when I shall not so often hear from the king. And all his subjects be very glad. I thank God, to be busy with the golf, for they take it for pastime; my heart is very good to it, and I am horribly busy making standards, banners, and bagets." The quaintly expressive phrase, "My heart is very good to it," remits to us a pleasant memory of a queen's grateful content with the sport which kept her subjects quiet and amused.

Unfortunately, we have little in the way of records for preserving the historical continuity of women golfers. From the same source as the above I get an entry taken out of the Dowager-Countess of Mars' House-book, under date September 23, 1638: "Paid for ane golf club to John the Baun 5s." Here is our introduction to a seventeenth-century player, but we are left to guess at the form and wood of that "ane club"; certes, it was what the noble lady would call finely fashioned and of most excellent workmanship; Master John Baun would see to that.

Of the game in the eighteenth century we read in a statistical account of Scotland, that the women of Musselburgh on holidays frequently play at golf; and I may possibly give the Scot a great shock by proving that the pot-hunting said to be so prevalent among the fair Saxons is a Scottish invention. We have no authentic account of women playing for aught but the love of the game, until incited thereto by the Musselburgh Golf Club. That primeval innocence should have no chance, you will note two handkerchiefs — silk ones — were added to the other premiums. The minute, dated December 14, 1810, runs : " The Club resolve to present by subscription a new Creel and Shawl to the best female golfer who plays on the annual occasion on 1st Jan. next, old style (12 Jan. new), to be intimated to the Fish Ladies by the Officer of the Club."

"Two of the best Barcelona silk handkerchiefs to be added to the above."

The account of this registered bribe lands us inside the door of the nineteenth century, and a few decades further, behold, we are in the middle of the ladies' links ! The invasion of England by Scottish gowff, *circa* the sixties, caused a rapid multiplication of clubs and courses. Woman caught the golf fever from the men, but the *habitat* of the male sufferer was put under strict quarantine, and a small piece of ground ornamented with a few greens and destitute of hazards, was presented to the ladies as a sufficient balm for their delirious energy ! From these undulating croquet lawns, plus a tee box and a few flags, have been evolved the short links of 1897. If we visit the courses of the earlier clubs we notice that they are always lengthening ; the bunkers deepen, other difficulties increase. Here and again we come across a rudimentary putting green, or hazard, but as months roll on they will disappear. When a new green is laid out there is always a struggle in its construction, between the tendency to preserve the ancestral type of croquet ground and the effort to adapt itself to the surrounding conditions of play. Why, with space and funds *ad libitum*, are many new links laid out on an improved model of thirty years ago, instead of being planned to fit the game of the best scratch players? These are often penalised by the structure of the course. The mean distance of the holes, or a badly placed hazard, may only allow them to reach the flag at the same time as their opponent to whom they give, perhaps, eighteen strokes. The player takes a half shot with cleek or iron and is on the green in one, and as the large handicap uses a higher tee and a full swing with a wooden club she is there also, and the better woman is one down. Again, at the next tee, scratch dares not take her driver, because the ball may run into the hazard placed to catch a weak second shot; neither approaching can she lay herself dead with a brassy, as the ball running up to the green will be caught in the bunker guarding it. She must therefore choose an iron, and with another short loft reach the flag in three. But the big handicap is by her side, for after her foozled drive, she used her wooden club to clear the second hazard, and a full iron enables her with her stroke to secure a half, though she does muff a short putt. The only thing to do is to smile and hide one's annoyance as best one can. Small wonder there are players for whom a medal round on some short courses is a better test of temper than golf!

The conditions which have improved our greens have been apparently the higher standard of play exhibited by women who have the advantage of constant rounds on the long links, and the greater increase of experience in matters connected with the sport. Though a player may not be sufficiently good to win a championship, yet she may know more about the game and the surroundings indispensable for its improvement, than a better golfer. It is chiefly stupidity and carelessness which hinder progress. More knowledge and enthusiasm are wanted, and these qualities are more general with the younger members who are not elected to club committees, where their elders, but not necessarily betters, have the vote.

There are sixty-four ladies' golf clubs upon record in England, thirty-two in Scotland, nine in Ireland, and three in Wales. It follows, therefore, we can only mention a few of the leading ones which are famous for longevity, a model green, or distinguished membership.

The most ancient woman's green, St. Andrews, 1867, is a putting course with eighteen holes. Already in 1875 Clark notes on prize days the largeness of the field and the fancy costumes of the competitors, remarking that on their own ground the best of the members would be backed freely against the cracks of the Royal and Ancient. A new course of twelve holes, varying in length from 150 to 300 yards, is now being laid out.

Westward Ho! founded in 1868. The members played between the Pebble Ridge and the present short and long links. It ceased to exist, but the gold challenge medal, engraved with a lady playing and the inscription, "The Westward Ho! and North Devon Ladies' Golf Club, 1868," attests its early origin. This trophy is a beautiful thing, very different from the Palais Royal rewards of modern clubs. However, some people prefer paste to gold. The new club started in 1894 has nine holes, with hazards of ditches and rushes.

The London Scottish Ladies', 1872, was reconstituted under the name of the Wimbledon Ladies' in 1890. The nine holes are bounded by the men's green. The chief hazard is inviolable furze, defended by tar lines. No skill is acquired in extricating the ball, which, if lying within the line, must be lifted and dropped with the loss of a stroke. I hear this local rule is to be revoked. It sounds too good to be true!

Pau, dating 1874, is one of the elderly clubs. Long driving and strong iron play are necessary for a good score round its nine holes.

The best players in Scotland have made North Berwick famous. Founded in 1888, it has now a membership of 300. Miss Gillies Smith has carried off the annual scratch medal eight times out of the eleven competitions.

The Prestwick St. Nicholas Ladies' have a good course, belonging formerly to the men, who handed it over when removing to new quarters in 1893. The Royal Belfast, 1888, is the most important green in Ireland, the County Down Ladies' Club, its formidable rival, not having links of their own, but using the long course. Women in Wales play little. At Penarth and Porthcawl they use the long course, but Rhyl has a separate links for ladies, and a distinguished member in Miss Kennedy.

Nothing can beat the eighteen holes owned by West Lancashire at Blundellsands. The distances between the tees and greens are arranged that every stroke tells; weakness and foozles are punished, and the good shot has its reward. The hazards are model; the club-house one of the best. Princes', a recent birth, is the only eighteen-hole course within a three and a half mile radius of Victoria Station, though extremely youthful, its management can give a third to many others. The links are difficult. They possess a grand supply of natural hazard in rush and whin; there are artificial bunkers and no tame hole. Very different in character is the course of Royal Eastbourne, a good and very favourite green, whose members are strong in numbers and quality. Blackheath must be remembered for its kind hospitality to guests, and a right interpretation of the laws and spirit of the game. It continuously improves its course on the common.

From the club we approach the player, and here it must be stated that while in Scotland a good orthodox style was prevalent in the earliest period, throughout the south, where golf was an exotic, style moulded chiefly on ignorance, or misapprehended theories, amused and appalled the few who had golfed north, or had enjoyed professional tuition. One of the chief characteristics of what we will call Early English golf was a hit with a cleek off a high tee, euphoniously termed driving! The attitudes assumed for a short approach consisted of angles—acute ones; the waggle, which had to be named before recognition, extended into a flowing, flamboyant tracery of the club-head over the entire tee, not the ball! Lady Margaret Hamilton Russell's appearances gave new ideas as to style and game; a full swing and better follow-through were cultivated. Such was the zeal of her imitators, that it was necessary afterwards to soften down and subdue the painstaking copies which bore so little mark of the original. Verticality and excess of swing are faults of southern golf, and were noticeable in the late championship; a good occasion for comparing the differences in Scottish and English form.

To enumerate a quarter of the good golfers would be impossible; the selection of a dozen who have appeared at the six championships is a difficult task; they are divided into two classes:

players of ten years or over, whose game is moulded, and those who have golfed a comparatively short while, and are still improving.

First, among the best exponents of a woman's game are the Misses Orr. They grew up with clubs in their hands. David Grant and North Berwick links trained hand and eye. They possess an unobtrusive, easy style, natural, accurate, scientific play, and a high reputation, which is but the *shadow* of their brilliant game. A countrywoman of theirs, Miss Sybil Whigham, was the best player at Portrush, in 1895. She also possesses the power of knowing what to do and how to do it. Her drives have a grand carry and run, and when in England she rarely meets an opponent worthy of her *steel*. Though Miss Whigham plays much at Cannes, the blue riband of the sport seems to have little attraction for her; were she only to appear more often it could not be denied her.

To Lady Margaret Hamilton Russell, who won the first three championships—a feat only surpassed by young Tommy, and equalled by the professionals Jamie Anderson and Bob Ferguson— English golfers owe more than has ever been acknowledged. A beautiful style, when combined with very fine play, leaves a mental photograph behind; and though it cannot be copied and reproduced as many think, being the result of physical and mental personality, it necessarily compels by attraction to a higher standard. Lady Margaret Hamilton Russell's appearances at the meetings of '93, '94, '95 were open object lessons to those who could use their eyes. The intrinsic beauty of her style will never be forgotten by those who have seen it.

Miss Lena Thomson has golfed since childhood. A very quiet style, and a deliberate swing, do not signal her form to a new "gallery." Though mistress of every club, her cleek shots and putting are the most telling points of the very good game she has always played.

A long experience of championships—for St. Anne's, Littlestone, Portrush, Hoylake, Gullane, Great Yarmouth, all admired her very pretty game—a thorough knowledge of golf, and continuous practice have not yet enabled Miss Issette Pearson to bring the coveted cup to the Wimbledon "Ladies'." *Tempus fugit!* Take the honour, most noble secretary! The "younger generation" are driving on the green.

The youngest of this younger generation, Miss

Lilian Smith, drives a fine ball too; she is a very possible future champion.

The feature of Miss Kennedy's game is her play with wooden clubs—no one gets away a better tee shot, or drives further through the green. There is an absence of effort and an ease in her style which pleases. More experience and confidence would strengthen her very fine game. The only English medallist among such players as the Misses Orr and Miss Titterton, she can be proud of her place in the semi-finals, and reasonably expect to add a gold medal to the bronze.

Miss M. Aitken, who began her golfing career with a half-swing, recently exchanged for a full one, has done a great deal in a short time. A constant player at North Berwick, and other centres which afford the best practice and example, with a natural turn for golf, she has every facility for reaching perfection. Only it requires time to make a champion.

Twice in the last three championships has Miss M. E. Phillips met and succumbed, after a good fight, to the eventual champion. Falling to the winner before the penultimate round be reached, is a piece of legitimate bad luck in the draw.

With fortune for her friend, the most consistent scorer and one of the best players in Kent and Surrey, must pass to a medal. Miss Phillips plays a particularly strong approach.

Miss A. Maxwell attracts attention. As match or score player she is equally good. Though put out by Miss Orr, there are few who can beat her in determination and consistency of game.

Miss Moeller, Elkley, is another young golfer; there is a dash and quickness of style here which appear ambitious of a win.

At the first Irish ladies' championship, Miss N. Graham was made a warm favourite, and justified public opinion by running into the finals; the following year, 1895, she reached the semi-finals, and 1896 saw her winner. A steady, cool player, she has come well to the front, and will have to be reckoned with at future meetings.

The ladies' championship originated in the wish expressed by a few members of Wimbledon to establish an annual open competition. Notices were sent out to other clubs, and on April 19, 1893, the Ladies' Golf Union was formed. The arrangement of the championship was amongst its primary objects. On June 13th, a field of 38 met at the short links of Lytham and

St. Anne's. Lady Margaret Hamilton Russell—at that time Lady Margaret Scott—being in a class by herself, won her four matches by 9 and 7, 8 and 7, 6 and 4, 7 and 5, and was declared champion. The long links at Littlestone were the scene of the 1894 meeting, and the specially arranged course a more severe test of the game. St. Anne's is a nine-hole green about 1 mile 350 odd yards in length, and its cops and bunkers are not to be compared with the more serious hazards at Littlestone; but here, again, the champion scored a second victory, though the competitors numbered 64, and a very marked improvement was visible in both play and style. At Portrush, May, 1895, Lady Margaret Hamilton Russell won for the third time in succession. The shortened course was rougher and more difficult than those of the preceding years: more luck was attached to the lies, and the half a dozen scratch competitors now amounted to ten. Comparing the large number of entries with the small number of first-class players, it is regrettable that so many ladies play who have not a 100 to 1 chance of reaching the finals. There must always be an element of luck in the draw, which is increased by these competitors, who could never come through their first heats were it not for the inferiority of many belonging to their own golfing status. Players who enter to gain the necessary nerve and experience to become winners may be below *par* in form, but they do not scratch to a formidable opponent, and they will make a fight; while those persons who enter for "the fun of it," as if golf were a picnic, or garden-party, swell the large total of "walk-overs" and "soft things," and disturb the chances of those who play for sport.

The Gullane meeting exhibited the finest golf played publicly by women. It vindicated to the most sceptic and captious critic their right to the name of golfers. Three out of the four honours fell to Scotland. Fifty-seven English were present, and only one reached the semi-finals; as the Scotch entry was thirty-five, and Ireland had ten representatives, the north appears more favourable for the production of winners than is England. The special good points of Scotch players are their full, easy swing, with an absence of pressing, their accurate iron play and sound putting. In the freedom of their strokes from sandy lies, and cleverness in bunkers, they far surpass the south, which is handicapped on its inland links by the want of suitable hazards.

Certainly, the north as a whole showed more *quality* in its game. Frequent matches with the other side of the Tweed would act most beneficially on our style and form. There was universal satisfaction over Miss E. C. Orr's win, and the capable and light-hearted way she achieved her victory.

Other champions are Miss Lena Thomson, Ireland — whom we have already mentioned — and Miss Hoyt, America, a young player from the Shinnecock Hills Club. Holland has also its championship, held by Miss Daisy de Brienen, a remarkably long and powerful driver. It is extremely difficult to obtain reliable information on woman's play abroad, and in the colonies, without having visited the links and seen the players. From what I have heard, I should imagine our scratch ladies could give the best players out of the British Isles, a third, but I have not sufficient data to form a decided opinion.

The Ladies' Golf Union, instituted 1893, was formed, among other reasons—(1) to promote the interests of the game of golf; (2) to obtain an uniformity of the rules of the game by establishing a representative legislative authority; (3)

THE LADIES' CHAMPIONSHIP CUP.

to establish an uniform system of handicapping; (4) to act as a tribunal and court of reference on points of uncertainty; (5) to arrange the Annual Championship Competition, and obtain the funds necessary for that purpose. All clubs on admission pay an entrance fee and yearly subscription, and are represented by a delegate at the meetings. The associated clubs now number twenty-seven. The bye-laws of the Union are :—1. In inter-club matches the minimum number of teams shall be eight for clubs of over 500 members, and six for clubs of 50 and under. 2. In inter-club matches each match won shall count two, in addition to the number of holes up.

This last is certainly an innovation, and was introduced to prevent jockeying a team; ladies having more faith in rule, than in honour, as a guard against abuses in sport. The Union has a President, Vice-Presidents, Hon. Treasurer, Hon. Secretary, and Hon. Auditor. What it sadly wants are a few old, first-class golfers, who, knowing all about the game from early childhood, would have an innate reverence and respect for its rules, customs, and traditions; and thus might be enabled to lead and control the well-intentioned but ignorant energy which would make a rule for every imaginable evil. It is always well when legislating to consider whether the new measure is an improvement on the former fault, or whether it has not attendant ills greater than the old. Our sex is more influenced by emotion than by motive; therefore let us proceed warily, when we try to improve on the honourable usages of the Royal and Ancient game!

Women do not waste their time on golf literature. The beauty of a first edition of Clark is unknown to them. You must not ask them if the first volume wholly dedicated to the ancient game be in prose or verse. I fancy only two ladies bought the Rev. John Kerr's lovely book on "Golf in East Lothian," though its price is not prohibitive. Mr. Horace Hutchinson is recognised by our sex in his character of golf *littérateur*, solely because, seven years ago, he had the temerity to challenge its driving capacities; and while tabooing its presence on the long links, generously welcomed it to a Jews' quarter! Out of gratitude for this invitation, and also perhaps because they never understand the Badminton Book on golf, ladies speak of him as "that man who writes." No, women do not invest half-crowns in professionals or books, yet, if a friend be interviewed on the links, they may buy the sixpenny apotheosis of her swing, including portrait in evening dress! But such things as the opening of new courses, professional matches, and information conveyed by "Tee Shots," can they not be read at the club for nothing? Is this, perhaps, the reason why the literature of ladies' golf has yet to be written? The author waits for readers. Some witty and original verses appear from time to time in "Golf," signed "Rose Champion de Crespigny," and of late years the *Golfing Annual* has included a paper by a lady golfer, so has the "Golfer's Guide." The *Badminton Magazine* has two papers by Mrs. Mackern, and *Hearth and Home* in 1896 published a special number to which women contributed. An hour's reading would finish, however, all that has been written on golf by our sex. The *Annual* of the Ladies' Golf Union is an official compilation of the society's regulations and meetings, with a list of the clubs and their members' names and addresses. It also contains reprints from sporting periodicals, but though a useful little work, is too much on the lines of a directory to be called literature. Yet if little be written much is reported. From the naïveté and boldness of her remarks, the golf paragraphist on a ladies' paper must possess a considerable handicap. Her unvarying admiration for new players and new links is exhaustless. To report a ladies' prize meeting *à l'ordinaire*, take a pound and a half of superlatives and mix in nine or ten good-sized personal compliments (open soapy ones preferred), sprinkle liberally with mistakes *re* score and quality of play, and colour with enthusiastic description of the pots won by the lucky hunters!

I have been asked to say a few words on the golf of the future. The links, as we have seen, are gradually assuming the character of the long courses, and we may observe a tendency to drive further with wood and iron. Thus we find the makings of a first-class game increasingly common among young players subjected to favourable conditions. These will drive much longer balls, be stronger with irons, play with more intuition and judgment than is done now. As woman increases her range of sport, the smaller golf competitions will decrease, while the championship will assume its full importance. Women will go to these meetings to *golf*, not to amuse themselves or others! The spirit of sport, which is the love of a thing for its own sake, unconditioned by personal advantage or pleasure, will gradually effect an improvement in everything connected with the game. The older players will have holed out, the younger, possessed of better physique and more sportsmanlike education, will develop to the utmost extent their capabilities for a pastime, where strength and force are not the chief essentials. The play of golfers like the Misses Orr, with the increasing prevalence of all conditions favourable to woman's athletic development, seems to justify the idea that the golfers of the future will have no short links, and though competing among themselves for championship honours, may use the long course with man, as they share with him the same lawn tennis court and hunting field.

APPENDIX.

THE CHAMPIONSHIP COURSES.

St. Andrews, 6,323 yards.

Holes.	Yards.	Holes.	Yards.
1	352	10	290
2	417	11	150
3	335	12	333
4	367	13	385
5	516	14	475
6	359	15	375
7	340	16	334
8	170	17	461
9	277	18	387
Out	3,133	In	3,190

Prestwick, 5,732 yards.

Holes.	Yards.	Holes.	Yards.
1	333	10	419
2	110	11	284
3	433	12	426
4	314	13	408
5	178	14	344
6	297	15	323
7	193	16	272
8	331	17	378
9	437	18	252
Out	2,626	In	3,106

MUIRFIELD, 5,890 yards.

Holes.	Yards.	Holes.	Yards.
1	205	10	250
2	365	11	425
3	330	12	355
4	330	13	310
5	465	14	150
6	310	15	275
7	300	16	520
8	330	17	280
9	320	18	370
Out	2,955	In	2,935

SANDWICH, 6,012 yards.

Holes.	Yards.	Holes.	Yards.
1	366	10	341
2	312	11	312
3	267	12	333
4	405	13	480
5	212	14	458
6	190	15	433
7	480	16	272
8	180	17	333
9	338	18	300
Out	2,750	In	3,262

HOYLAKE, 5,955 yards.

Holes.	Yards.	Holes.	Yards.
1	350	10	335
2	300	11	180
3	480	12	340
4	155	13	110
5	370	14	460
6	350	15	410
7	195	16	400
8	440	17	350
9	350	18	380
Out	2,990	In	2,965

WINNERS OF THE OPEN CHAMPIONSHIP.

Year	Winner	Score	Venue
1860.	W. Park, sen.	174	at Prestwick
1861.	Tom Morris, sen.	163	,, ,,
1862.	Tom Morris, sen.	163	,, ,,
1863.	W. Park, sen.	168	,, ,,
1864.	Tom Morris, sen.	160	,, ,,
1865.	A. Strath	162	,, ,,
1866.	W. Park, sen.	169	,, ,,
1867.	Tom Morris, sen.	170	,, ,,
1868.	Tom Morris, jun.	154	,, ,,
1869.	Tom Morris, jun.	157	,, ,,
1870.	Tom Morris, jun.	149	,, ,,

In 1870, the Champion Belt presented by the Prestwick Club in 1860, became the absolute property of young Tom Morris, in virtue of his having won it three times in succession. There was no competition in 1871, but in 1872, the "Royal and Ancient," the "Honourable Company," and the Prestwick Club presented the present Championship Cup for annual competition.

Year	Winner	Score and Venue
1872.	Tom Morris, jun.	166, at Prestwick.
1873.	Tom Kidd	179, at St. Andrews.
1874.	Mungo Park	159, at Musselburgh.
1875.	Willie Park, sen.	166, at Prestwick.
1876.	Bob Martin	176, at St. Andrews.
1877.	Jamie Anderson	160, at Musselburgh.
1878.	Jamie Anderson	157, at Prestwick.

1879. Jamie Anderson ... 170, at St. Andrews.
1880. Bob Ferguson ... 162, at Musselburgh.
1881. Bob Ferguson ... 170, at Prestwick.
1882. Bob Ferguson ... 171, at St. Andrews.
1883. Willie Fernie ... 159, at Musselburgh.
 (After a tie with Bob Ferguson.)
1884. Jack Simpson ... 160, at Prestwick.
1885. Bob Martin ... 171, at St. Andrews.
1886. D. Brown ... 157, at Musselburgh.
1887. W. Park, jun. ... 161, at Prestwick.
1888. Jack Burns ... 171, at St. Andrews.
1889. W. Park, jun. ... 155, at Musselburgh.
 (After a tie with Andrew Kirkaldy.)
1890. Mr. John Ball, jun.... 164, at Prestwick.
1891. Hugh Kirkaldy ... 166, at St. Andrews.
(In 1892 the competition was extended to 72 holes.)
1892. Mr. H. H. Hilton ... 305, at Muirfield.
1893. W. Auchterlonie ... 322, at Prestwick.
1894. J. H. Taylor ... 326, at Sandwich.
1895. J. H. Taylor ... 322, at St. Andrews.
1896. Harry Vardon ... 316, at Muirfield.
 (After a tie with J. H. Taylor.)
1897. Mr. H. H. Hilton ... 314, at Hoylake.
1898. Harry Vardon ... 307, at Prestwick.

WINNERS OF THE AMATEUR CHAMPIONSHIP.

1886. Mr. H. G. Hutchinson beat Mr. H. A. Lamb by 7 up and 6 to play, at St. Andrews.
1887. Mr. H. G. Hutchinson beat Mr. John Ball, jun., by 1 hole, at Hoylake.
1888. Mr. John Ball, jun., beat Mr. J. E. Laidlay by 5 up and 4 to play, at Prestwick.
1889. Mr. J. E. Laidlay beat Mr. L. Balfour-Melville by 2 up and 1 to play, at St. Andrews.
1890. Mr. John Ball, jun., beat Mr. J. E. Laidlay by 4 up and 3 to play, at Hoylake.
1891. Mr. J. E. Laidlay beat Mr. H. H. Hilton by 1 hole, after a tie, at St. Andrews.
1892. Mr. John Ball, jun., beat Mr. H. H. Hilton by 3 up and 1 to play, at Sandwich.
1893. Mr. P. C. Anderson beat Mr. J. E. Laidlay by 1 hole, at Prestwick.
1894. Mr. John Ball, jun., beat Mr. S. Mure Fergusson by 1 hole, at Hoylake.
1895. Mr. L. Balfour-Melville beat Mr. John Ball, jun., by 1 hole, after a tie, at St. Andrews.
1896. Mr. F. G. Tait beat Mr. H. H. Hilton by 8 up and 7 to play, at Sandwich.
1897. Mr. A. J. T. Allan beat Mr. J. Robb by 4 up and 2 to play, at Muirfield.
1898. Mr. F. G. Tait beat Mr. S. Mure Fergusson by 7 up and 6 to play, at Hoylake.

X

WINNERS OF THE LADIES' CHAMPIONSHIP.

1893. Lady Margaret Scott beat Miss Issette Pearson by 7 up and 5 to play, at St. Anne's.
1894. Lady Margaret Scott beat Miss Issette Pearson by 3 up and 2 to play, at Littlestone.
1895. Lady Margaret Scott beat Miss E. Lythgoe by 5 up and 4 to play, at Portrush.
1896. Miss Amy Pascoe beat Miss L. Thomson by 3 up and 2 to play, at Hoylake.
1897. Miss E. C. Orr beat Miss Orr by 4 up and 3 to play, at Gullane.
1898 Miss Lena Thomson beat Miss E. Nevile by 6 up and 5 to play, at Great Yarmouth.

WINNERS OF THE IRISH AMATEUR (OPEN) CHAMPIONSHIP.

1892. Mr. Alex. Stuart, at Portrush.
1893. Mr. John Ball, jun., at Newcastle, Co. Down.
1894. Mr. John Ball, jun., at Dollymount.
1895. Mr. W. B. Taylor, at Portrush.
1896. Mr. W. B. Taylor, at Newcastle. Co. Down.
1897. Mr. H. H. Hilton, at Dollymount.

APPENDIX.

AGE OF LEADING GOLF CLUBS.

	Established.
Royal Blackheath Golf Club	1608
Edinburgh Burgess Golfing Society	1735
Honourable Company of Edinburgh Golfers	1744
Royal and Ancient Golf Club of St. Andrews	1754
Bruntsfield Links Golf Club	1761
Royal Musselburgh Golf Club	1774
Royal Aberdeen Golf Club	1780
Crail Golfing Society	1786
Glasgow Golf Club	1787
Burntisland Golf Club	1797
Montrose Golf Club (now Royal Albert)	1810
Manchester Golf Club	1818
Innerleven Golf Club	1820
Royal Perth Golfing Society and County and City Club	1824
Calcutta Golf Club	1829
Montrose Academy Golf Club	1832
North Berwick Golf Club	1832
Carnoustie and Taymouth Golf Club	1839
Royal Bombay Gymkhana Golf Club	1842
Panmure Golf Club, Monifieth	1845
Leven Thistle Golf Club	1846
Lanark Golf Club	1851
Prestwick Golf Club	1851
Prestwick St. Nicholas Golf Club	1851
Tantallon Golf Club, North Berwick	1853

APPENDIX.

	Established
Cupar Golf Club ...	1855
Dunbar Golf Club ...	1856
Bruntsfield Allied Golf Club ...	1856
Pau Golf Club ...	1856
Earlsferry and Elie Golf Club ...	1858
Warrender Golf Club ...	1858
King James VI. Golf Club, Perth ...	1859
East Lothian Golf Club...	1859
Royal North Devon Golf Club ...	1864
London Scottish Golf Club ...	1865
Royal Wimbledon Golf Club ...	1865
Royal Liverpool Golf Club, Hoylake ...	1869
Montreal Golf Club ...	1873
Great Yarmouth Golf Club ...	1882
St. George's Golf Club, Sandwich ...	1887
Royal West Norfolk Golf Club, Brancaster ...	1892

GLOSSARY.

Addressing the Ball—The player's method of standing and handling the club preparatory to striking the ball.

All Even—An expression used to describe the position or result of a match when neither side has gained any advantage. *See* HALVED.

All Square—Synonymous with *All Even*.

Approach—The stroke by which the ball is played on to the putting green.

Baff—To play a ball high into the air with a backward spin.

Baffing Spoon or Baffy—A short wooden club with a deeply lofted face, formerly used for playing approaches.

Bents—The long wiry grasses found on sea-shore links.

Bisque—A point taken by the receiver of odds at any period during the game.

Blind Hole or Hazard—A *blind hole* is one of which the putting-green is not visible to the player as he plays his shot. A *blind hazard* is a hazard which is hidden from his view.

Bogey—A method of scoring by holes against an imaginary opponent. The number of strokes which ought to be taken to each hole without serious mistakes.

Bone—The piece of horn, vulcanite, or other material let into the sole of wooden clubs to protect the lower edge of the face.

Borrow—To play a ball up or down a hill or slope, instead of straight at the hole, so that the slope will cause the ball to return towards the hole.

Brassy—A wooden club soled with brass.

Break Club—Any hard object lying near the ball, which might break the club in the act of striking.

Bulger—A convex-faced club.

Bunker—Originally a natural sand-hole on the golf course. Now used also of artificially made hazards with built-up faces.

Bye—The hole or holes of the stipulated course that remain unplayed, after a match is finished.

Caddie—The boy or man who carries the player's clubs, tees his ball, and from whom he takes advice.

Carry—The distance which a ball travels from the club face to the spot where it first alights on the ground.

Cleek—An iron club with a long and narrow face—used for long shots through the green when a ball lies badly or when a wooden club would take it too far.

Club—Any legitimate implement used in striking the ball.

Course—the ground within the limits of which the game is played.

Cup—Any small indentation on the ground.

Cut—To put right-hand or backward spin on the ball so as to check its rolling forward after its fall.

Dead—A ball is said to lie *dead* when it lies so near the hole that the player is certain to hole it in the next stroke. A ball is also said to "fall dead" when it does not roll after reaching the ground.

Divot—The slice of turf cut out by the club in playing a stroke.

Dormy—A player is said to be *dormy* when he is as many holes up as there remain to be played, so that he cannot be beaten, and at the worst must halve the match.

Down—A player is said to be *down* when his opponent has won one or more holes than he has.

Draw—Synonymous with *Pull*.

Driver—The wooden club used for playing the longest strokes.

Duff—To hit the ground so far or so deep behind the ball that the ball only travels a short distance.

Face—The hitting surface of a club-head.

Fog—Thick mossy grass.

Follow-through—The forward following of the club after hitting the ball.

Foozle—Any thoroughly bad stroke short of missing the ball altogether.

Fore!—The word shouted by the golfer when about to strike to give warning to parties in front.

Fore-caddie—The boy who precedes the players to show the line to the hole and to mark where the balls lie.

Full Shot—A shot played with a full swing, and intended to travel as far as possible.

Gobble—A ball played too hard at the hole which nevertheless goes in.

Green—Synonymous with *Links* or *Course*; also used as a contraction for *putting green*.

Grief—When a player has played his ball into a hazard of any description he is said to be in *grief*.

Grip—First, the upper part of the club shaft gripped by the player; second, the manner of gripping the club; third, a narrow ditch on the course used as a drain.

Gutty—A gutta-percha golf ball.

Half-one—A handicap of one stroke at every second hole.

Half shot—A shot played with a half swing, and not intended to go as far as a full shot.

Halved—A halved hole is one to which both sides have taken the same number of strokes. A match is halved when no advantage has been gained on either side.

Hanging ball—A ball which lies on a downward slope in the direction in which it has to be driven.

Hazard—Any kind of difficulty, not being the ordinary grass of the course, into which a golf ball may get, with the exceptions mentioned in Rule 15.

Heel—First, the part of the face or hitting surface of the club-head nearest the shaft; second, to hit the ball with the heel so as to cause it to fly to the right.

Hole—First, the entire space of ground between the teeing ground and the hole; second, the hole itself; third, to play the ball into the hole.

Hole High—A ball is said to be *hole high* when it has been played as far as the hole, but not necessarily on to the putting green.

Home—A ball is said to be *home* when it is played on to the putting green from a distance.

Honour—The privilege of playing first from the tee.

Hook—To pull the ball round to the left with the toe of the club. Synonymous with *Pull* and *Draw*.

Horn—*See* BONE.

Hose—The Hose or socket is that part of the head of an iron club into which the shaft is fitted.

Iron—A club with an iron head, used chiefly for approaching the hole and for lifting the ball over obstacles.

Jerk—To play a ball so that the club-head strikes into the ground after hitting the ball.

Lie—The position of a ball anywhere on the course after it has been played.

Lift—To take a ball out of a hazard and drop it or tee it according to the Rules.

Like—To play *the like* at a given hole is to play a stroke which equalises the number played by the opposite side.

Links—The ground on which the game is played.

Loft—To raise a ball into the air.

Lofter—An iron club used to loft the ball.

Made—A player is said to be *made* when he is within a full shot of the green.

APPENDIX. 313

Mashie—An iron club which is shorter in the head than the iron.

Match play—The method of playing a game of golf by counting the number of holes gained or lost by each side.

Medal play—The method of playing a game of golf by counting the number of strokes taken to the round by each side.

Miss the globe—An expression used to describe the failure of a player to move the ball at all, after striking at it.

Neck—The curved part of the head next the shaft.

Niblick—An iron club with a round, small, and very heavy head, used when great force is necessary to extract a ball from its position.

Nose—The end of the head farthest from the shaft.

Odds—To play the odds, at a given hole, is to play one stroke more than the opposite side.

One off two, one off three, &c.—When the opposite side has played two or three strokes more, the other side plays "one off two" or "one off three" as the case may be.

Par—The par of a hole or round is the total number of strokes which should be required for them without mistakes.

Press—To put an extra amount of force into the swing.

Pull—Synonymous with *Draw* or *Hook*.

Putt—A stroke played with a putter on the putting green with the object of playing the ball into the hole.

Putter—A club with either a wooden or metal head, used on the putting green to play the ball into the hole.

Putty—A golf ball made of composition.

Quarter shot—A shot played with a quarter swing from the wrists.

Round—A term used to describe a game over the whole course.

Run—First, the distance a ball travels after alighting on the ground; second, to make the ball travel along the ground instead of lofting it.

Scare—The part of the club where the head and shaft are joined.

Sclaff—To scrape the surface of the ground with the sole of the club-head before striking the ball.

Scratch player—A good player, who receives neither handicap nor penalty.

Set—The player's equipment of clubs.

Shaft—The handle of the club.

Short game—Approaching and putting.

Slice—To draw the face of the club across the ball so that it curves to the right.

Socket—*See* HOSE.

Sole—The flat part of the club-head which rests on the ground.

Spoon—A wooden club with a lofted face.

Spring—The elasticity of the club shaft.

Stance—The position of the player's feet in playing a stroke.

Steal—A long putt holed unexpectedly.

Stymie—A stymie occurs on the putting green when one of the balls lies directly in front of the other on the line to the hole, and the balls are more than six inches apart.

Swing—The method in which the club is swung in the act of striking.

Swipe—A full shot.

Tee—The small elevation, usually a pinch of sand, from which the ball is struck for the first stroke to each hole.

Teeing-ground—The marked-out space from which the ball must be struck at the commencement of each hole.

Third—A handicap of one stroke given at every third hole.

Toe—Synonymous with *Nose*.

Top—To hit the ball above its centre.

Up—A player is said to be *up* when he has gained one or more holes upon his opponent.

Wrist shot—A short stroke played with the wrists.

RULES FOR THE GAME OF GOLF ADOPTED BY THE ROYAL AND ANCIENT GOLF CLUB OF ST. ANDREWS, 1891.

1. The Game of Golf is played by two or more sides, each playing its own ball. A side may consist of one or more persons.

2. The game consists in each side playing a ball from a tee into a hole by successive strokes, and the hole is won by the side holing its ball in the fewest strokes, except as otherwise provided for in the rules. If two sides hole out in the same number of strokes, the hole is halved.

3. The teeing ground shall be indicated by two marks placed in a line at right angles to the course, and the player shall not tee in front of, nor on either side of, these marks, nor more than two club lengths behind them. A ball played from outside the limits of the teeing ground, as thus defined, may be recalled by the opposite side.

The hole shall be 4¼ inches in diameter, and at least 4 inches deep.

4. The ball must be fairly struck at, and not pushed, scraped, or spooned, under penalty of the loss of the hole. Any movement of the club which is intended to strike the ball is a stroke.

5. The game commences by each side playing a ball from the first teeing ground. In a match with two or more on a side, the partners shall strike off alternately from the tees, and shall strike alternately during the play of the hole.

The players who are to strike against each other shall be named at starting, and shall continue in the same order during the match.

The player who shall play first on each side shall be named by his own side.

In case of failure to agree, it shall be settled by lot or toss which side shall have the option of leading.

6. If a player shall play when his partner should have done so, his side shall lose the hole, except in the case of the tee shot, when the stroke shall be recalled at the option of the opponents.

7. The side winning a hole shall lead in starting for the next hole, and may recall the opponent's stroke should he play out of order. This privilege is called the "honour." On starting for a new match, the winner of the long match in the previous round is entitled to the "honour." Should the first match have been halved, the winner of the last hole gained is entitled to the "honour."

8. One round of the Links—generally 18 holes—is a match, unless otherwise agreed upon. The match is won by the side which gets more holes ahead than there remain holes to be played, or by the side winning the last hole when the match was all even at the second last hole. If both sides have won the same number, it is a halved match.

9. After the balls are struck from the tee, the ball furthest from the hole to which the parties are playing shall be played first, except as otherwise provided for in the rules. Should the wrong side play first, the opponent may recall the stroke before his side has played.

10. Unless with the opponent's consent, a ball struck from the tee shall not be changed, touched, or moved before the hole is played out, under the penalty of one stroke, except as otherwise provided for in the rules.

11. In playing through the green, all *loose* impediments, within a club length of a ball which is not lying in or touching a hazard, may be removed, but loose impediments

which are more than a club length from the ball shall not be removed under the penalty of one stroke.

12. Before striking at the ball, the player shall not move, bend, or break anything fixed or growing near the ball, except in the act of placing his feet on the ground for the purpose of addressing the ball, and in soling his club to address the ball, under the penalty of the loss of the hole, except as provided for in Rule 18.

13. A ball stuck fast in wet ground or sand may be taken out and replaced loosely in the hole which it has made.

14. When a ball lies in or touches a hazard, the club shall not touch the ground, nor shall anything be touched or moved before the player strikes at the ball, except that the player may place his feet firmly on the ground for the purpose of addressing the ball, under the penalty of the loss of the hole. But if in the backward or in the downward swing, any grass, bent, whin, or other growing substance, or the side of a bunker, a wall, paling, or other immovable substance be touched, no penalty shall be incurred.

15. A " hazard " shall be any bunker of whatever nature : —water, sand, loose earth, mole hills, paths, roads or railways, whins, bushes, rushes, rabbit scrapes, fences, ditches, or anything which is not the ordinary green of the course, except sand blown on to the grass by wind, or sprinkled on grass for the preservation of the Links, or snow or ice, or bare patches on the course.

16. A player or a player's caddie shall not press down or remove any irregularities of surface near the ball, except at the teeing ground, under the penalty of the loss of the hole.

17. If any vessel, wheelbarrow, tool, roller, grass-cutter, box, or other similar obstruction has been placed upon the course, such obstruction may be removed. A ball lying on or touching such obstruction, or on clothes, or nets, or on ground under repair or temporarily covered up or opened, may be lifted and dropped at the nearest point of the

course, but a ball lifted in a hazard shall be dropped in the hazard. A ball lying in a golf hole or flag hole may be lifted and dropped not more than a club length behind such hole.

18. When a ball is completely covered with fog, bent, whins, &c., only so much thereof shall be set aside as that the player shall have a view of his ball before he plays, whether in a line with the hole or otherwise.

19. When the ball is to be dropped, the player shall drop it. He shall front the hole, stand erect behind the hazard, keep the spot from which the ball was lifted (or in the case of running water, the spot at which it entered) in a line between him and the hole, and drop the ball behind him from his head, standing as far behind the hazard as he may please.

20. When the balls in play lie within six inches of each other—measured from their nearest points—the ball nearer the hole shall be lifted until the other is played, and shall then be replaced as nearly as possible in its original position. Should the ball further from the hole be accidentally moved in so doing, it shall be replaced. Should the lie of the lifted ball be altered by the opponent in playing, it may be placed in a lie near to, and as nearly as possible similar to, that from which it was lifted.

21. If the ball lie or be lost in water, the player may drop a ball, under the penalty of one stroke.

22. Whatever happens by accident to a ball *in motion*, such as its being deflected or stopped by any agency outside the match, or by the fore caddie, is a "rub of the green," and the ball shall be played from where it lies. Should a ball lodge in anything moving, such ball, or, if it cannot be recovered, another ball shall be dropped as nearly as possibly at the spot where the object was when the ball lodged in it. But if a ball *at rest* be displaced by any agency outside the match, the player shall drop it or another ball as nearly as possible at the spot where it

lay. On the putting green the ball may be replaced by hand.

23. If the player's ball strike, or be accidentally moved by an opponent or by an opponent's caddie or clubs, the opponent loses the hole.

24. If the player's ball strike, or be stopped by himself or his partner, or either of their caddies or clubs, or if, while in the act of playing, the player strike the ball twice, his side loses the hole.

25. If the player when not making a stroke, or his partner or either of their caddies touch their side's ball, except at the tee, so as to move it, or by touching anything cause it to move, the penalty is one stroke.

26. A ball is considered to have been moved if it leave its original position in the least degree and stop in another; but if a player touches his ball and thereby cause it to oscillate, without causing it to leave its original position, it is not moved in the sense of Rule 25.

27. A player's side loses a stroke if he play the opponent's ball, unless (1) the opponent then play the player's ball, whereby the penalty is cancelled, and the hole must be played out with the balls thus exchanged, or (2) the mistake occur through wrong information given by the opponent, in which case the mistake, if discovered before the opponent has played, must be rectified by placing a ball as nearly as possible where the opponent's ball lay.

If it be discovered before either side has struck off at the tee that one side has played out the previous hole with the side of a party not engaged in the match, that side loses that hole.

28. If a ball be lost, the player's side loses the hole. A ball shall be held as lost if it be not found within five minutes after the search is begun.

29. A ball must be played wherever it lies, or the hole be given up, except as otherwise provided for in the rules.

30. The term "putting green" shall mean the ground within 20 yards of the hole, excepting hazards.

31. All loose impediments may be removed from the putting green, except the opponent's ball, when at a greater distance from the player's than six inches.

32. In a match of three or more sides, a ball in any degree lying between the player and the hole must be lifted, or, if on the putting green, holed out.

33. When the ball is on the putting green, no mark shall be placed, nor line drawn as a guide. The line to the hole may be pointed out, but the person doing so may not touch the ground with the hand or club.

The player may have his own or his partner's caddie to stand at the hole, but none of the players or their caddies may move so as to shield the ball from, or expose it to, the wind.

The penalty for any breach of this rule is the loss of the hole.

34. The player or his caddie may remove (but not press down) sand, earth, worm casts or snow lying around the hole or on the line of his putt. This shall be done by brushing lightly with the hand only, across the putt and not along it. Dung may be removed to a side by an iron club, but the club must not be laid with more than its own weight upon the ground. The putting line must not be touched by club, hand, or foot, except as above authorised, or immediately in front of the ball in the act of addressing it, under the penalty of the loss of the hole.

35. Either side is entitled to have the flag-stick removed when approaching the hole. If the ball rest against the flag-stick when in the hole, the player shall be entitled to remove the stick, and, if the ball fall in, it shall be considered as holed out in the previous stroke.

36. A player shall not play until the opponent's ball shall have ceased to roll, under the penalty of one stroke. Should the player's ball knock in the opponent's ball, the latter

APPENDIX.

shall be counted as holed out in the previous stroke. If, in playing, the player's ball displace the opponent's ball, the opponent shall have the option of replacing it.

37. A player shall not ask for advice, nor be knowingly advised about the game by word, look, or gesture from any one except his own caddie, or his partner or partner's caddie, under the penalty of the loss of the hole.

38. If a ball split into separate pieces, another ball may be put down where the largest portion lies, or if two pieces are apparently of equal size, it may be put where either piece lies, at the option of the player. If a ball crack or become unplayable, the player may change it, on intimating to his opponent his intention to do so.

39. A penalty stroke shall not be counted the stroke of a player, and shall not affect the rotation of play.

40. Should any dispute arise on any point, the players have the right of determining the party or parties to whom the dispute shall be referred; but should they not agree, either party may refer it to the Green Committee of the green where the dispute occurs, and their decision shall be final. Should the dispute not be covered by the Rules of Golf, the arbiters must decide it by equity.

SPECIAL RULES FOR MEDAL PLAY.

1. In Club competitions, the competitor doing the stipulated course in fewest strokes shall be the winner.

2. If the lowest score be made by two or more competitors, the ties shall be decided by another round to be played either on the same or on any other day as the Captain, or, in his absence, the Secretary shall direct.

3. New holes shall be made for the Medal Round, and thereafter no member shall play any stroke on a putting green before competing.

4. The scores shall be kept by a special marker, or by the competitors noting each other's scores. The scores marked shall be checked at the finish of each hole. On

completion of the course, the score of the player shall be signed by the person keeping the score and handed to the Secretary.

5. If a ball be lost, the player shall return as nearly as possible to the spot where the ball was struck, tee another ball, and lose a stroke. If the lost ball be found before he has struck the other ball, the first shall continue in play.

6. If the player's ball strike himself, or his clubs or caddie, or if, in the act of playing, the player strike the ball twice, the penalty shall be one stroke.

7. If a competitor's ball strike the other player, or his clubs or caddie, it is a "rub of the green," and the ball shall be played from where it lies.

8. A ball may, under a penalty of two strokes, be lifted out of a difficulty of any description, and be teed behind same.

9. All balls shall be holed out, and when play is on the putting green, the flag shall be removed, and the competitor whose ball is nearest the hole shall have the option of holing out first, or of lifting his ball, if it be in such a position that it might, if left, give an advantage to the other competitor. Throughout the green a competitor can have the other competitor's ball lifted, if he find that it interferes with his stroke.

10. A competitor may not play with a professional, and he may not receive advice from any one but his caddie.

A fore caddie may be employed.

11. Competitors may not discontinue play because of bad weather.

12. The penalty for a breach of any rule shall be disqualification.

13. Any dispute regarding the play shall be determined by the Green Committee.

14. The ordinary Rules of Golf, so far as they are not at variance with these special rules, shall apply to medal play.

ETIQUETTE OF GOLF.

The following customs belong to the established Etiquette of Golf, and should be observed by all Golfers :—

1. No player, caddie, or onlooker should move or talk during a stroke.
2. No player should play from the tee until the party in front have played their second strokes and are out of range, nor play to the Putting-Green till the party in front have holed out and moved away.
3. The player who leads from the tee should be allowed to play before his opponent tees his ball.
4. Players who have holed out should not try their putts over again when other players are following them.
5. Players looking for a lost ball must allow any other match coming up to pass them.
6. A party playing three or more balls must allow a two-ball match to pass them.
7. A party playing a shorter round must allow a two-ball match playing the whole round to pass them.
8. A player should not putt at the hole when the flag is in it.
9. The reckoning of the strokes in match play is kept by the terms :—" The odd," "two more," "three more," &c., and "one off three," "one off two," "the like." The reckoning of the holes is kept by the terms :—So many "holes up," or "all even," and so many "to play."
10. Turf cut or displaced by a stroke in playing should be at once replaced.

TABLE SHOWING PROPORTION OF MEDAL HANDICAP ALLOWED IN MATCH PLAY.

For singles, three-fourths of difference between handicap allowances.
In foursomes, three-eighths of difference of aggregate handicap allowances on either side.
A half-stroke, or over, counts as one. Smaller fractions do not count.

Difference	Strokes in Singles	Strokes in Foursomes	Difference	Strokes in Singles	Strokes in Foursomes	Difference	Strokes in Singles	Strokes in Foursomes
1	1	0	13	10	5	25	19	9
2	2	1	14	11	5	26	20	10
3	2	1	15	11	6	27	20	10
4	3	2	16	12	6	28	21	11
5	4	2	17	13	6	29	22	11
6	5	2	18	14	7	30	23	11
7	5	3	19	14	7	31	23	12
8	6	3	20	15	8	32	24	12
9	7	3	21	16	8	33	25	12
10	8	4	22	17	8	34	26	13
11	8	4	23	17	9	35	26	13
12	9	5	24	18	9	36	27	14

DIRECTORY OF LEADING GOLF CLUBS.

The Royal and Ancient Golf Club.—Club House, St. Andrews, N.B. Entrance Fee, £15; Annual Subscription, £3. Hon Sec., C. S. Grace, Esq., The Club House.

The Honourable Company of Edinburgh Golfers.—Club House, Muirfield, East Lothian, N.B. Entrance Fee, £12 12s.; Annual Subscription, £3 3s. Hon. Sec., A. G. G. Asher, Esq., W.S., 18, Hill Street, Edinburgh.

Prestwick Golf Club.—Club House, Prestwick, Ayr, N.B. Entrance Fee, £15; Annual Subscription, £2. Hon. Sec. and Treas., Harry Hart, Esq., 5, Fort Street, Ayr.

Royal Liverpool Golf Club.—Club House, Hoylake, Cheshire. Entrance Fee, £10 10s.; Annual Subscription, £3 3s., Secretary, W. Ryder Richardson, Esq., The Club House.

KENT.

St. George's Club, Sandwich.—Club House, Sandwich, Kent. Entrance Fee, £15 15s.; Annual Subscription, £3 3s. Hon. Sec., W. Rutherford, Esq., 3, Plowden Buildings, Middle Temple, London, E.C.

Littlestone Golf Club.—Club House, Littlestone. Entrance Fee, £10 10s.; Annual Subscription, £1 1s. Hon. Sec. and Treas., H. E. Johnson, Esq., 23, Knightsbridge Street, London, E.C.

Cinque Ports Golf Club, Deal.—Club House, Deal, Kent. Entrance Fee, £5 5s.; Annual Subscription, £3 3s. Hon. Sec. and Treas., Lieut.-Col. Hungerford, Walmer, Deal.

SUSSEX.

Brighton and Hove Golf Club.—Club House, Hove, Brighton. Entrance Fee, £5 5s.; Annual Subscription, £2 2s. Hon. Sec., H. J. Percival, Esq., The Club House.

Seaford Golf Club.—Club House, Seaford. Entrance Fee, £5 5s.; Annual Subscription, £2 2s. Sec. and Treas., T. Gilroy, Esq., Bay Hotel, Seaford.

Rye Golf Club.—Club House, Rye. Entrance Fee, £5 5s.; Annual Subscription, £2 2s. Hon. Sec., H. S. Colt, Esq., 33, Havelock Road, Hastings.

SUFFOLK.

Aldeburgh Golf Club.—Club House, Aldeburgh. Entrance Fee, £5 5s.; Annual Subscription, £1 1s. Hon. Sec., John Fry, Esq., The Club House.

Felixstowe Golf Club.—Club House, Felixstowe. Hon. Sec., J. Hutchison Driver, Esq., The Club House.

NORFOLK.

Royal West Norfolk Golf Club, Brancaster.—Club House, Brancaster. Entrance Fee, £5 5s.; Annual Subscription, £1 1s. Hon. Sec., W. H. Simms Reeve, York Cottage, Brancaster.

Royal Norwich Golf Club.—Club House, Norwich. Entrance Fee, £2 2s.; Annual Subscription, £1 11s. 6d. Hon. Sec., C. Steward, Esq., King Street House, Norwich.

Royal Cromer Golf Club.—Club House, Cromer. Entrance Fee, £5 5s.; Annual Subscription, £2 2s. Hon. Sec., P. M. Lucas, Esq., Cromer.

CORNWALL.

Royal Cornwall Golf Club.—Club House, Bodmin, Cornwall. Entrance Fee, £1; Annual Subscription, £1. Hon. Sec., H. Young Jamieson, Esq., St. Petrocks, Bodmin.

YORKSHIRE.

Scarborough Golf Club.—Club House, Ganton. Entrance Fee, £2 2s.; Annual Subscription, £2 2s. Hon. Sec., F. Bedwell, Esq., 32, Queen Street, Scarborough.

NORTHUMBERLAND.

Alnmouth Golf Club.—Club House, Alnmouth. Entrance Fee, £2; Annual Subscription, £1. Hon. Sec., J. de C. Paynter, Esq., Belvidere, Alnwick.

ISLE OF WIGHT.

Royal Isle of Wight Golf Club.—Club House, Bembridge. Entrance Fee, £5 5s.; Annual Subscriptions, £2 2s. Hon. Sec., Davenport Knight, Esq., Club House.

CHANNEL ISLANDS.

Royal Jersey Golf Club.—Club House, St. Heliers. Entrance Fee, £2 2s.; Annual Subscription, £1 10s. Hon. Sec., Capt. T. S. Robin, 4, Claremont Terrace, Jersey.

Royal Guernsey Golf Club.—Club House, l'Ancresse Vale, Guernsey. Entrance Fee, £3 3s.; Annual Subscription, £1 10s. Hon. Sec., T. S. Dobree, Esq., Club House.

IRELAND.

Royal Dublin Golf Club.—Club House, Dollymount. Entrance Fee, £8 8s.; Annual Subscription, £2. Hon. Sec., G. C. May, Esq., 13, Fitzwilliam Square, Dublin.

Royal Portrush Golf Club.—Club House, Portrush. Entrance Fee, £5 5s.; Annual Subscription, £1 1s. Hon. Sec., J. M. Russell, Esq., 25, Mark Street, Portrush.

LONDON GOLF CLUBS.

Royal Blackheath Golf Club.—Club House, Blackheath. Entrance Fee, £5 5s.; Annual Subscription, £3 3s. Hon. Sec., W. G. Barnes, Esq., 93, Blackheath Hill, S.E.

Royal Wimbledon Golf Club.—Club House, Wimbledon Common. Entrance Fee, £10 10s.; Annual Subscription, £3 3s. Hon. Sec., N. R. Foster, Esq., 1, Sunnyside, Wimbledon.

London Scottish Golf Club.—Club House, Wimbledon Common. Entrance Fee, £5 5s.; Annual Subscription, £2.

Balham Golf Club.—Entrance Fee, £3 3s.; Annual Subscription, £3 3s. Hon. Sec., A. Cole, Esq., Oak Lodge, Telford Park.

Beckenham Golf Club.—Entrance Fee, £5 5s.; Annual Subscription, £3 3s. Hon. Sec., P. G. Collins, Esq., 21, The Avenue, Beckenham.

Chiswick Golf Club.—Entrance Fee, £2 2s.; Annual Subscription, £4 4s. Hon. Sec., E. H. Laurie, Esq., 21, Earl's Court Square, S.W.

Craven Park Golf Club.—Entrance Fee, £1 1s.; Annual Subscription, £1 10s. Hon. Sec., Dr. H. J. Buck, 23, Clapton Common, N.E.

Dulwich and Sydenham Hill Golf Club.—Entrance Fee, £5 5s.; Annual Subscription, £3 3s. Hon. Sec., J. McNab, Esq., The Club House.

Ealing Golf Club.—Annual Subscription, £4 4s. Hon. Sec., A. T. W. McCaul, 21, St. Helen's Place, Bishopsgate Street, E.C.

East Finchley Golf Club.—Entrance Fee, £1 1s.; Annual Subscription, £3 3s. Hon. Sec., J. W. P. Scott, Esq., 17, North Road, Highgate, N.W.

Eltham Golf Club.—Club House, Eltham. Entrance Fee, £10 10s.; Annual Subscription, £5 5s. Sec. and Treas., R. A. Collingwood, Esq., The Club House, Eltham, Kent.

Royal Epping Forest Golf Club.—Club House, Chingford, Essex. Entrance Fee, £3 3s.; Annual Subscription, £1 1s. Sec., T. F. Caldwell, Esq., Queen's Grove Road, Chingford.

Finchley Golf Club.—Entrance Fee, £2 2s.; Annual Subscription, £2 2s. Hon. Sec., A. F. Drew, Esq., 22, Cyprus Road, Finchley, N.

Hampstead Golf Club.—Entrance Fee, £5 5s.; Annual Subscription, £3 3s. Hon. Sec., H. Knox, Esq., The Club House.

Honor Oak and Forest Park Golf Club.—Annual Subscription, £4 4s. Hon. Sec., W. Wingate, Esq., 37, Mark Lane.

Mid-Surrey Golf Club.—Club House, Old Deer Park, Richmond. Entrance Fee, £10 10s.; Annual Subscription, £5 5s. Sec. and Treas., J. C. Montgomerie, Esq., The Club House.

Muswell Hill Golf Club.—Entrance Fee, £3 3s.; Annual Subscription, £2 2s. Hon. Sec., D. A. Watson, Esq., Tottenham Wood House, Wood Green.

Neasden Golf Club.—Club House, Neasden, N.W. Entrance Fee, £5 5s.; Annual Subscription, £6 6s. Hon. Sec., S. Clifford, Esq., The Club House.

Norbury Golf Club.—Entrance Fee, £2 2s.; Annual Subscription, £3 3s. Hon. Sec., A. W. Macfarlane, Esq., 34, Kempshott Road, Streatham, S.W.

Prince's Golf Club.—Club House, Mitcham. Entrance Fee, £6 6s.; Annual Subscription, £4 4s. Hon. Sec., R. Hippesly Cox, Esq., The Club House.

Raynes Park Golf Club.—Annual Subscription, £3 3s. Joint Hon. Secs., F. W. Butler, Esq. and W. H. Glanville, Esq., The Club House.

Richmond Golf Club.—Club House, Sudbrooke Park, Richmond. Entrance Fee, £10 10s.; Annual Subscription, £5 5s.

Romford Golf Club.—Club House, Romford, Essex. Entrance Fee, £4 4s.; Annual Subscription, £2 2s. Hon. Sec., W. H. Bose, Esq., Golf Club, Romford.

Stanmore Golf Club.—Club House, Stanmore, Middlesex. Entrance Fee, £5 5s.; Annual Subscription, £4 4s. Sec., C. Adams, Esq., Stanmore, Middlesex.

Tooting Bec Golf Club.—Club House, Furzedown, Balham. Entrance Fee, £15 15s.; Annual Subscription, £3 3s.

Wanstead Park Golf Club.—Club House, Wanstead Park, Essex. Entrance Fee, £3 3s.; Annual Subscription, £3 3s. Hon. Sec., F. W. Rawlinson, Esq., Deepdene, Snaresbrook, Essex.

West Drayton Golf Club.—Entrance Fee, £3 3s.; Annual Subscription, £3 3s. Hon. Sec., A. T. Tallent, Esq., 4, Field Court, Gray's Inn, W.C.

The Incorporated West Herts Golf Club.—Club House, Cassiobury Park, Watford. Entrance Fee, £7 7s.; Annual Subscription, £4 4s. Sec., Ernest R. Harby, Esq., Greenhill Lodge, Watford.

West Middlesex Golf Club.—Club House, Hanwell. Entrance Fee, £7 7s.; Annual Subscription, £5 5s. Hon. Sec., W. Jackson, Esq., The Club House.

Willesden Golf Club.—Entrance Fee, £2 2s.; Annual Subscription, £3 3s. Hon. Sec., B. Pierpoint, Esq., 44, Plympton Road, Brondesbury, N.W.

Oldest Established American Golf Clubs.

St. Andrews, Yonkers	1888
Shinnecock Hills Golf Club...	1890
Brookline (Boston)	1892
Newport	1892-93
Tuxedo...	1893
Essex (Mass.)	1893
Chicago	1893-94

UNWIN BROTHERS, THE GRESHAM PRESS, WOKING AND LONDON.

www.ingramcontent.com/pod-product-compliance
Lightning Source LLC
Chambersburg PA
CBHW020311240426
43673CB00039B/777